My Pagan Ancestor Zuri

A Parallel Journey: Christchurch to Stonehenge

My Pagan Ancestor Zuri

A Parallel Journey: Christchurch
to Stonehenge

Ken West

Winchester, UK
Washington, USA

JOHN HUNT PUBLISHING

First published by Chronos Books, 2019
Chronos Books is an imprint of John Hunt Publishing Ltd., No. 3 East St., Alresford,
Hampshire SO24 9EE, UK
office@jhpbooks.com
www.johnhuntpublishing.com
www.chronosbooks.com

For distributor details and how to order please visit the 'Ordering' section on our website.

Text copyright: Ken West 2018

ISBN: 978 1 78904 155 2
978 1 78904 156 9 (ebook)
Library of Congress Control Number: 2018946926

A CIP catalogue record for this book is available from the British Library.

Design: Stuart Davies

UK: Printed and bound by CPI Group (UK) Ltd, Croydon, CR0 4YY
US: Printed and bound by Thomson-Shore, 7300 West Joy Road, Dexter, MI 48130

We operate a distinctive and ethical publishing philosophy in
all areas of our business, from our global network of authors to
production and worldwide distribution.

Contents

Chapter 1: A Handshake across Time   1

Chapter 2: The Gerontocracy   10

Chapter 3: Fecund Heathens   15

Chapter 4: Avonlands   21

Chapter 5: Utility of the Picturesque   29

Chapter 6: The Food Factory   37

Chapter 7: A Day in the Life of...   49

Chapter 8: The Fall of the Pagans   60

Chapter 9: Celestial Sisters   72

Chapter 10: Bearing in Bear Country   78

Chapter 11: To Us a Pagan Child is Born   86

Chapter 12: A Place of our Own   91

Chapter 13: Pagan Pods   100

Chapter 14: Paradise Lost   106

Chapter 15: The Fruit of Paradise   110

Chapter 16: The Joy of Movement   113

Chapter 17: The Avon Legacy   118

Chapter 18: The Nature of Acquisition   126

Chapter 19: Flint 'n' Bone 'n' Stone   133

Chapter 20: To the Temple   139

Chapter 21: Temple of the Sun   151

Chapter 22: The Advent of Bling   155

Chapter 23: The Ill Wind   162

Chapter 24: The Innocent Blue Tit   167

Chapter 25: Feeding the Birds   177

Chapter 26: Postscript   181

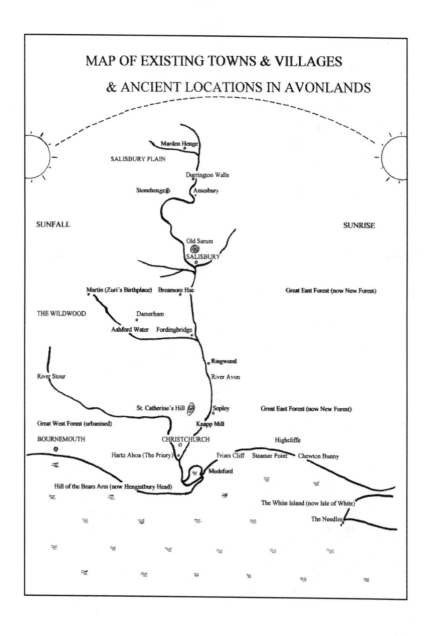

MAP OF EXISTING TOWNS & VILLAGES
& ANCIENT LOCATIONS IN AVONLANDS

Chapter 1

A Handshake across Time

A warrior lies adrift in my Christchurch street, recumbent and silent; the only resident in possession of a plot with no postcode. In truth, he never needed post because he could neither read nor write, yet his predecessors built a wondrous Temple that we now call Stonehenge. I first met him, so to speak, when I purchased a bungalow a few doors from him. He lies in a neat, green space, our most aged resident; a prehistoric nestled amongst our pensioner properties. The grassed space is no more than 100 paces long. In the centre is a small mound, covered by a mass of low growing shrub called Rose of Sharon, its rampant periphery shaved into a neat circle by council mowers. This pretend shrubbery is a Bronze Age tomb. I imagine myself devising a myth in which this assumed warrior would suddenly rise up and out of his dark grave, resurrected. He would stand there, short at 167 centimetres yet imposing, a roe deerskin over his shoulder, the haft of a bronze dagger peeking out from his waist and the shaft of a glistening spear in his right hand. He would look at me and speak: I would not understand a word he says.

This warrior, like me, represents change, an unstoppable sequence, where people come and people go, perhaps 125 generations from me to this man. He was about 80 generations after those of his kin who began building at Stonehenge. He has a high probability of being related to me and carrying some of my genes yet he speaks a foreign language, almost certainly a form of Basque. His forebears brought the language with them when they left their ice age retreat down in what we now call Spain. His tribe is my tribe yet I know it not; he lived here, as I do.

It was not by accident that my wife Ann, and I, along with this Bronze Age warrior, chose to live in this little spot of Christchurch in the English county of Dorset. Nature brought our ancestors here as the Ice Age retreated over 12,000 years ago; who were they? It struck me as strange that we know more about Egypt and the pharaohs than we know about our own forebears. We, and they, came here because of the sea. We for leisure, for pretty scenery, for the good life, a bolt hole from the vicissitudes of London life with its toxic air that kills thousands each year. It is our wealthy pensioner retreat. They followed the coast, seeking a place to eke out a living, to hunt and forage for food. Later, they farmed and then traded, and needed a sheltered place for their boats. Everything points to Hengistbury Head as that early site, where silver haired people now walk their dogs. The Head is a shapely peninsular curving around a soft sandy beach landing; a home recognisable from way out at sea.

I often look out over to Hengistbury, aware that archaeological excavations in recent years in the Channel Islands and Isles of Scilly have changed our view of how people first populated this coast. After the Ice Age, people moved north along the French coast, probably as hunters on foot, as logboats had yet to be invented. That coast was still joined to the English side, although it was further out than now. Over time, the glaciers melted and as the sea rose, it flooded the Channel and separated England from Europe. It also isolated the Channel Islands from the French coast and flooded much of the Isles of Scilly, creating the islands we know today. The people experienced all this and knew precisely where the islands and mainland were situated. By 3000 BC, these sea people had created a maritime region which archaeologists now call the Western Seaways. It included the Belgian and French coast down to Brittany, the English south coast, the Channel Isles, the Isles of Scilly and the Irish east coast, extending up to the Scottish Islands. These people traded, most probably furs, shells, flint, stone from Europe and fish.

All the earliest civilisations developed along a navigable river, what we now term riverine cultures. The reasons are not hard to appreciate because movement over land was difficult and waterways represented the superhighway. On a river, it was difficult to become lost and there was ample water to drink and fish and wildfowl to eat. But, leave the waterway, step into the dense forest and feel the tension rise; the land is dangerous. Not only are you potentially lost within a few miles but there is the danger of attack by bears and wolves and perhaps by unfriendly hunters.

But, there are rivers and there are rivers, so it begs the question as to what is the ideal for a riverine culture? Imagine the need; a calm, navigable, deep river that stretches well inland, without rapids or rocks and with extensive marshes and wetland areas full of birdlife. The length of the river is critical, especially when farming begins, because if it drains just the lands controlled by the tribe then warfare is avoided. Otherwise, extracting too much water upstream to irrigate fields deprives those lower down. They might also foul the water for those downstream. The essential need is for friable, alluvial, silt soils alongside the river so that plants have water beneath them in the summer to grow green and lush, the typical English water meadow. These possess soils that are light enough to be farmed by human labour and without the more efficient metal tools and ploughs that will arrive much later. Ideally, the river opens out into a sheltered bay, with warm shallow seawater for fishing and safe harbouring. There would be extensive forested areas to each side of the river, for hunting and the supply of wood, perhaps the forest stretching to infinity. Rarely, there might be chalk downs up the river, only lightly wooded, with trees like ash that can be felled with flint tools, unlike the much harder oak whose nemesis is to be the metal axe. The chalk soil, unlike heavy clays, can be dug using antler picks. The exposed pure white chalk may well have been a sign of purity to these early people. And surely, if the Gods favoured them then they would place the river running north to south, so the sun warms the valley as it sweeps across in a perfect arc, rising in the east and setting in the west.

You might have realized that I have just described the local River Avon; an exceptional river, the liquid lifeblood watering the perfect tribal land. As a chalk river, it reacts slowly to wet weather and does not flash flood like rivers on clay, such as the Thames or the Severn. The floods are more gentle, adding fertility and calcium carbonate, which sweetens soil, to the water meadows where the people farm. Nowhere along the south coast do these elements come together as abundantly as on the River Avon and its close neighbour the River Stour. Few people appreciate these facts as they drive across the causeway into Christchurch and give the sinuous River Avon a sideways glance on their way to the supermarket. But our ancestors, as farming began, saw the massive food potential of these rivers, little of which we notice today.

Ann and I, having lived all over England and Wales, retired here and felt an immediate affinity. Here, away from the familiarity of my home ground, my senses are stimulated. I possess none of that familiarity often noted in the locals, that inability to see the colour and scent wafting on the unchanging and routine breeze. The local museum, the castle, even the scenery, inspires me whilst it is so often ignored by those who have always lived here, the familiar wallpaper that can never be recalled. When I drift into a new place, I sense my disconnect and then work hard to create, to foster, a new attachment. Christchurch, which attracts many wealthy pensioners from all over Britain, is relatively welcoming, being used to new blood. Nobody here calls me an offcomer, which is good. That was my experience up North, where the locals worry about dissipated newcomers with fancy ideas, especially those from down South.

I walk and muse, and sleep and muse, and wake up with notes to write down, subsumed in thought about these ancient people, my kinfolk. Finally, I decide that I need to create an advocate for the tribe, a person who lived where I live, a neighbour separated by thousands of years, but what date do I choose? The people were all hunter-gatherers 10,000 years ago and we know little about them. Yet millennia later they are building great Temples like Stonehenge and creating the beautiful artefacts that now fill our museums. My preferred date, in the Neolithic period, slowly awakes in me. Should this advocate, also my alter ego, be a man or a woman? Our current knowledge of these early periods suggests that the men were the farmers yet still hunted for meat. Being active, they are most likely to give the writer exciting scenarios even though this period appears to have a low incidence of conflict. Men, though, are rather one dimensional. The action man is all machismo and vanity, his stories related to his libido and hunting, and male communication skills are often poor. In contrast, a woman is more social, more family orientated, more inclined to speak to those around her, to discuss tribal issues, to ponder, to see the wider picture. In talking to children and imparting skills, women are now considered to have been the arbiters of language, perhaps even the inventors of language. Today, we see women as possessing more emotional intelligence than men, the so called soft skills of communication and harmonious relationships. In Neolithic society, the communal nurturing of children appears to have been through women. Children were more like little adults and invaluable members of the work team. The men were graduating to farming, with hunting less successful as the game was pushed out by the increasing population in this area. Their society also seems to have maintained a balance of power betwixt men and women; even if the word power is not a word they understand. As evidence of this, analysis proves that a high percentage of women, and children, were interred under the bluestones at Stonehenge. They were all cremated prior to burial and appear to have been members of an elite. Archaeology in general appears to be favouring a gender balance in those early days. This suggests that there was no warrior culture, at least until much later, when my Bronze Age neighbour was interred.

I decide that my fleshed out ghost from the past is to be a woman in her teens, who will bear a child, and is perhaps half way through her allotted span of thirty to forty years; no three score and ten for her so she will not have to fear dementia. Her name is Zuri, the Basque word for white. White, chalk white, shell white, is a sacred colour and when Zuri was born her skin was unusually light. She lives in the Late Neolithic period, the end of the New Stone Age, when that period meets the Bronze Age, in 2200 BC. She has the blue eyes of the hunter-gatherers, a mutation from a single European individual from the Black Sea region. Farming has arrived in Britain as part of the biggest social change the world has ever seen. It appears, in Britain at least, a period in which there was little warfare and a high degree of cooperation. By working together, or force of will, or belief, great Temples and henges were built. Zuri lived in a successful and vibrant society at its peak, yet change was coming and, to use the cliché, things will never be the same again. I decide that Zuri cannot be a narrator because she does not understand facts or chronological sequence. Even the Greek word 'histor', to judge, will not be written down for a further 2000 years. She is bright eyed, quizzical, about 153 centimetres tall, slim and lithe, as are all her tribe; nobody is overweight. Zuri looks you in the eye and possesses that native stature, that nobility of movement that Thomas Hardy, in later Dorset, would call spry. She is tanned by the sun and weather beaten by the salt laden sea and the winds. It is a colour that millennia later will define which women have high status, namely, the white skinned ones. This thought reminds me that when I was young, in the 1960s, I used Spanish holidays to create a new post war status; the suntan. Forty years later, skin cancer has changed my perspective.

Zuri belongs to this land, to this water, to this place, far more than I or a modern person ever could. She lived here and I live here, thousands of years of human life and I sit at the head, albeit only until I die. Zuri's blood is my blood but has a different character. She was attached to a placenta wholly nurtured by water, fish, plants and meat from within the land actually visible from her mother's hut. Likewise, her mother suckled her on breast milk powered from the immediate surroundings. Zuri's body was formed from the very land and water upon which they stood, walked and floated. She knows little of inland Britain, much of which is densely forested. She assumes that we are an island, in part because she knows her people came across the sea from the land where the traders come from. I doubt that she is aware that her Neolithic tribe are pioneers, constantly pushing new farming technology. As I create and vocalize Zuri, sometimes using her native Basque language, I am aware that she and her tribe were far more conscious of the living universe than modern people. I must struggle to understand her mythology and how she might use plants and animals. I need to be empathic, to understand and share her feelings. Yet she has no writing, no dictionary and converses with me in a very limited vocabulary. She is also very superstitious. To her, everything is in the lap of the Gods. Forgive me; I can only write down what facts exist about the Neolithic, a few meagre dots on a page, and fill in the space between the dots using fiction, what some writers would call faction. I could try to validate this approach, to justify it, by referring to archaeologist Colin Renfrew, who called this approach cognitive archaeology. That is a hard call and, ultimately, this is an imagined biography, of an unknown Neolithic woman, literally a handshake across time.

So, I have a new neighbour called Zuri. Her hut was on the promontory, near the centre of Christchurch, where the station now lies on rails that link it to Brussels and Paris. Rest assured that such a woman lived, had children, and died. Her children knew no school and, unlike today, respected their elders from

7

whom they learned their life skills. Like me, she ate fish, plants and meat, made love, argued, but, unlike me, she experienced periods and childbirth. Unlike me, had she remained childless it would have been catastrophic for her. A barren womb would have been a punishment by the Gods and it would have given her sleepless nights.

In my world, I have no children and I do not have to fear retribution. I can count myself along with the growing numbers of people who do not conceive, of single people and those who are gay and lesbian plus the increasing number of women who prefer a career to family. In contrast to Zuri's society, the world has no need of more children and it is a trend that benefits society. We pay our taxes, don't need the state to educate our children and divert those resources into the community. Even those who have children find that they have nurtured wanderers because they increasingly go to university and do not return, they find a life elsewhere. The parents, like me, grow old, and if they can afford it, they have a habit of clustering in favoured retirement places, like Christchurch. Here, I like to call our grey haired mass the gerontocracy, a dominant body of old people, mostly affluent old people but more about them later.

If we, the childless, created a different world then it is also a decision that has social consequences. Zuri, embraced within her community, could not comprehend the absence of family. Perhaps it is all about ifs. If I am widowed then I am alone. Alone, I will die unattended and not with "his family around his bedside" as the obits so often rather smugly state. Even the media have their one-liners ready for the occasion with that graphic headline "Lonely man lies dead in bungalow for 3 weeks."

Zuri would struggle to understand my community and its idle leisure. What would she make of my street in 2017, where virtually nobody rises to go to paid work and quietness rules until after nine each morning. I love my walk along the coast from Friars Cliff to Chewton Bunny and back, which I do most days each week. It is a sensory walk, the audio theme the lapping murmur at the edge of the sea; there is always sea sound, loud or not too loud. Then there is the odour, the ozone, the decomposing seaweed; another constant. As for vision, I see what I choose to see, and every day I see the old and mortality confronts me. Widows and widowers, lone people; companion dogs, canine surrogates for the lost partner; public seats with memorial plaques recording that he or she "Loved this place", and covertly placed cremated remains, snuck into a corner or slipped over the quay edge at Mudeford; a wreath or bunch of flowers, so often exotic vulnerable orchids exposed to brutal salt winds, an anniversary token to past good times, to companionship.

This mortality is the antithesis of the beach life that surrounds me, with its disinterested vitality, the furious energy of toddlers with buckets and spades, litter bins stuffed with disposable barbecue trays, charcoal in the sand, nappy liners stuffed under bushes; the joy of laughter. All this reminds me of our liberty, our ability to choose what we want to do, where we want to live, whether to have or not to have children, even to choose to be alone. That is the real gulf between now and Zuri's time, for she must conform, must do what everybody else does, think like everybody else does. It is time for her to meet the gerontocracy.

Chapter 2

The Gerontocracy

It would be a mistake to think that tribes no longer inhabit Christchurch. I am an honorary member of the biggest and most politically influential tribe in Britain, the gerontocracy. My membership is by virtue of being old so it costs me nothing other than arthritis and creaking joints; my membership lapses the moment I stop breathing.

The word tribe needs to be better defined because my usage is not the way Zuri might use it. The dictionary suggests that it is a social division of a people, especially a preliterate people, defined in terms of common descent, territory and culture. Today, she would be shocked to see how kinship means little in Christchurch and yet territory and culture still define who and what we are. Since her time, politics, and variations in wealth and age, have redefined what we mean by tribal.

The gerontocracy is dominant in Christchurch because the town has the oldest population in the country. I feel powerful, we feel powerful, because the political parties fear us; they know that we take the trouble to vote. So they protect the National Health Service, pensions, the cold weather fuel payments, free eye tests and the bus that we use to get to the opticians. We have the power and they pander to us. If membership is automatic due to age, then having money is what makes the cultural difference; the affluent pensioner is a force to reckon with, all about me, me, me. The gerontocracy is recognisable because it dresses tribally, formally, conservatively, perhaps in German manufactured clothing. The men prefer the short back and sides. The women might occasionally show a little excess. I noted an elderly woman wearing two leopard skins; one the hat and one the coat. The blessing, assuming them to be real, was that they did not match so were not siblings. I could imagine Zuri experiencing mass envy at the sight of such beautiful skins. She would not believe them to be manufactured. My membership of the tribe might be spurious; I sometimes wear overalls as a journeyman gardener. This is letting the side down and betrays my proletarian background. I am aware that the true gerontocratic dresses up to garden, a smart shirt, even a tie, whilst the ladies may favour a summer frock while sporting a stainless steel trowel. We can still be territorial as the garden tends to stop when it reaches the footpath. The path and kerb remains the zone of the proletariat, the council staff. Our neatest gardens can have the scruffiest kerbs.

The Christchurch gerontocracy tends to vote Conservative, not universally, but by and large. They are often self-made, down from London, or town, as they would say. A Mercedes or Audi may sit in the immaculate garage, the floor perhaps painted, and they will abjure public transport. Their wider territory is easily identified because it contains bungalows and retirement apartments. Typically, the large house bought for the growing family becomes a liability when children leave and "Independent, Safe and Secure Retirement Living" is required. The sales blurb, written by a marketeer aware that the male, according to statistics, will die first, goes on to describe a feminine nirvana, as a new widow resident states that "A month after moving in, I fulfilled a lifelong dream to visit the Taj Mahal in India." This was, according to the salesman, because she was freed from the "responsibilities of a large house and the worries of living alone." The attraction of having a retirement home is that it's more about being out of it rather than in it; the ability to walk out and leave it safely empty. Apartments spring up in the town centre, with no need for a garage or parking space, and are too expensive for the young to buy. They promote sales by offering a free car, which conflicts with the sales blurb that they are designed for members of the gerontocracy stripped of their driving licence. Perhaps it's because we can't find the car keys, as it's a fine line between independence and Alzheimer's. The entire area could be seen by the young as a massive coastal care home with silver haired people, sitting behind windows, staring out to sea.

Perhaps we are archetypical Christchurch residents, Ann and I. A typical resident will have moved here from London using their city purchasing power to intrude into the area, pushing up house prices and consequently denying youngsters their opportunity to buy a property; or so the argument goes. There are streets and streets in Christchurch full of tribal bungalows full of people like us. There are even estate agents that sell only bungalows, and they emphasize how their properties are disability friendly and close to "well surfaced paths."

In the Bronze Age, they defined their territory around Christchurch by interring their elite in mounded tombs, such as in my street and along St Catherine's Hill. We now do this by placing teak memorial benches, with a pseudo bronze plaque as its memento mori, a reminder of a life and a death. The inscription inevitably informs the readers about somebody else who loved this place, or loved the view, or spent many pleasant times hereabouts. The plaque never states "The tribal lands are lovely but too damn expensive."

I have no doubt that Zuri would be amazed at the way we live today and she would be puzzled by the way in which the gerontocracy can be regarded by society. We can be perceived as an inconsequential liability because we don't spend recklessly or use credit to boost the economy; the past was always a better place. Our politicians can see us as recumbent bodies lying in wait to bleed the resources of the National Health Service. Our state pension, earned over a lifetime of paying taxes, is now called a benefit, one of the many draining the exchequer. We are not considered as a functioning part of society, more an aged abutment, a bureau of volunteers, an unpaid army of mentors, child carers, of artists and knitters. We are also the mainstays of that principal British social institution, the garden centre. Stewarts, on the north edge of Christchurch, is a centre of excellence in that regard. It has masses of paraphernalia in the form of gifts, conservatory furniture and pictures, and is overlooked by a fine restaurant. Almost as an oversight, it is a purveyor of plants. For certain, at Christmas, reindeer are much easier to find than plants; just follow the nose. Needless to say, I am a Privilege Card holder for this establishment; there is no greater delight than the Dexter meat pie at Stewart's. Dexter is the beef, not the chef.

The Conservatives have a party political broadcast running as I write this. Previous members of the proletariat, having abandoned the Labour Party, are featured recounting their middle class desires for the future of their children. They must have a good education, a home of their own, employment that they enjoy, never to be bored, an ability to pay their debts and most importantly, not to have to wear overalls. Finally, the parents did not want their children to have to worry about them in later life.

It's almost farcical, this desire to disenfranchise children of their future and the benefits that accrue from hardship and failure. It is these experiences, the stress, pain, loss and anxiety, effectively life in the 1940s and 1950s, which make the gerontocracy what they are. Sadly, and contrary to my argument, they proved to be spoilers because they wielded their power, voted for Brexit and the young have a changed future. We momentously voted out but with no intellectual clue as to where to go, or how to get there.

The joy of Friars Cliff is the walk's straight out and along the coast; no need for a car. I appreciate that, as a member of the gerontocracy, my walk is an indulgent muse. I look out to sea and I visualize the proposed Navitas wind turbines, hundreds of them, the wind farm destined to spoil the horizon for the gerontocracy, and they voted against them. I look at walkers coming towards me and I say "good morning" and they don't reply. So many people are cheerless. Am I threatening; an older solo male and too friendly? It is anxiety, the curse of our times. Everybody seems anxious and an unseen army of counsellors and psychotherapists, very evident in Christchurch, has arisen in recent decades to de-stress their clients.

I often pick up some litter on my return and the black plastic bags contain dog poop. The dirty hand is the left one, the one that picks up the poop bags and the foul looking white tissues and choc bar wrappers. Who are these people, why do they dump stuff like this? A despotic urge builds and I consider how I would respond should I witness the act of littering. Closer to home, the council have erected another row of beach huts looking out to the Needles, and they have for sale notices on them. Where will it end; will the entire coastline be fringed by huts? Why, are beach huts, posh sheds, considered enhancing whereas wind turbines out at sea are deemed ugly? Amazingly, 4000 years after Zuri's time we are still building huts on the beach. I realize that it is time for me to regain my focus, to tease out what we know about the Neolithic. Our knowledge of prehistory would be weaker if it was not for the people who actually came face to face with these early tribes. Their empire gave us the name Britannia; it is time to meet the Romans.

Chapter 3

Fecund Heathens

The Romans, when they invaded Dorset, filled in some of the spaces between the dots in my story. In their actions and in their writing, they tell us a little about how tribal development had occurred in this country. In asking what the Romans did for us we should also be asking what the Neolithic did for the Romans. Why did the Romans invade, not once but twice? They had to amass an invasion fleet, both costly and a distraction from their other territorial issues in Europe. It is evident that they wanted what England had to offer, that the area appealed to them as it had to Zuri's forebears.

The Romans, dominant in mainland Europe, were always aware of our island and gave it the Latin name Britannia, even though it was less a country and more a confederation of tribal areas. They first invaded the South East under Julius Caesar in 54 BC but had to withdraw due to uprisings in Europe. The South East of Britannia remained Romanized for about 100 years before Aulus Plautius and, slightly later the same year, Emperor Claudius, invaded in AD 43. It took about 20 years to subdue what we call England and Wales. That gave them control of the fertile land, the grain, the wealth of England with perhaps half an eye on copper, tin and lead deposits. The poor land in Ireland and Scotland meant they took little or no interest in those countries. The Romans consolidated Britannia at Hadrian's Wall and the soldiers who built this were Dalmatian immigrants, rather like the gerontocracy using the Polish workers to build extensions and conservatories.

The invasion began in the Romanized South East, and the Legions moved west, attacking from the coast at Wareham and advancing up to Dorchester. On the way, they must have overrun

Hengistbury Head and Christchurch, but we have no evidence of that. Overall, they appear to have beaten the local tribes with little difficulty. Yet I must take care in case my narrative might sanitize the situation, suggesting that the civilising Romans were necessarily beneficial. Typically, they will have suppressed the tribes by giving them vassal status, a subservience that meant the men were effectively enslaved and the Romans then owned the land. Mary Beard, the historian, talks of female rape as a Roman preoccupation because the soldiers, all virile young men and banned from marriage, will have taken their pick of the women. There was no crime in rape as the women were considered the property of a man and the beaten men no longer owned their property. The pick of the women may have been forced into military prostitution, treated as slaves or concubines. Overall, killing was not the Roman way, as they required grain, skins and ores and needed the people to maintain production. Following defeat, Dorset, with few strategically important Roman towns or ores to mine, was left to fall back to agrarian life, ultimately under the yoke of the Roman farm and villa.

It is evident that resistance to the invasion could lead to a violent end. A skeleton of a British warrior is an exhibit in Dorchester Museum and there is a ballista bolt neatly embedded in his vertebrae. It must have been horrendously painful, this iron spear shot by a type of crossbow. He was defending perhaps the most populated hillfort in Britain, Maiden Castle, against the Romans. One thing, oops, two things the Romans did for us were, firstly, to record the name of the tribe living in Dorset, including this dead warrior, namely the Durotriges, phonetically pronounced as dur o tree gaz. This name probably gave us the word Dorset. The second thing the Romans did was to end pre-history and for many, British history started when they arrived. Nothing is recorded in writing prior to the Romans and all we have is what remains in the prehistoric landscape. Yet the Romans arrived 2000 years ago, a full 2200 years after Zuri lived here. She and her tribe were no closer to the Durotriges than we are so we must reflect on how much changed over those 2000 years of prehistory.

In writing this, I now realize how ignorant I have been. In the past I saw the hillforts such as Maiden Castle, the burial mounds, even Stonehenge, as contemporaneous, of the same period. Yet the Durotriges built the hillforts in the Iron Age, starting around 500 BC. The tribe became prominent as a consequence of the farming expansion brought about by the introduction of the iron plough, and perhaps draft animals. The hillfort was, in truth, a social consequence, a safe area into which the farmers could retreat. It was necessary because the evidence suggests that by the Iron Age tribal rifts had become commonplace, probably in the form of cattle raids.

There were no hillforts over 2000 years earlier, when Zuri's ancestors built Stonehenge. It was a further 1000 years before the Bronze Age tombs appeared, and another 1000 years before the hillforts began. What this tells us is that her people survived and prospered in this area and ultimately became the Durotriges. This hides the fact that as the population grew, people and with them power, moved around the area and then across Britannia. Over this period, the population outstripped the productive land on the Avon and moved to broader areas of land around places like Maiden Castle and Hod Hill, on the River Stour. Yet, even this became too small an area to maintain a growing population. Late in the period, when the iron plough arrived, tribes in the East and the Midlands, those who lived on rich clay soils were able to exploit this land. These Iron Age tribes experienced population growth and tribal power moved to these areas, where Boudicca and the Iceni tribe put up perhaps the only effective resistance to the Romans. The Durotriges continued to live in Dorset, in a receding agrarian economy that itself protected the hillforts and monuments against development, leaving them relatively intact to this day.

The Romans were on my mind as Ann and I walked over to Badbury Rings, an amazing hillfort intersected by two Roman roads. This tells us that it was a regional centre for the Durotriges and had to be subdued. A cuckoo called, a rare sound today. The bird was nonplussed because it needed trees and the only trees were around the hillfort, a wooded island in a grain prairie. Up high on the fort I looked out over the chalk downs and realized that, up to Victorian times and Hardy's Wessex stories, Dorset had been little more than a massive sheep farm from the time of the Roman villa. For more than 2000 years, a person might have walked unimpeded across this open sward. Zuri's people knew it before then, when the chalk soils supported a mass of plant species, many of them food plants, all of which later succumbed to the land maggots, otherwise called sheep. The Naturalist J.E. Lousley, in his seminal book *Wild Flowers of Chalk and Limestone* noted the paucity of flora in Dorset due to sheep grazing as early as the 1940s. At least it remained as grassland, covered in sheep dung, insects and birds including a lot more cuckoos. That changed as late as the 1950s, when artificial fertilizers came to the fore and it turned into an extensive grain prairie, relatively dead for wildlife and with the field run-off polluting the water in the Stour and Avon.

Another thing the later Romans did for us, after they adopted Christianity, was to disparage paganism. Did this attitude ultimately prevent us revering our pagan history simply because it was not Christian? In a Christian culture I am left with real concerns about the word pagan. It sits in a raw spot in the national psyche because recorded history tells us that the Venerable Bede and St Cuthbert revitalized the British by dismissing our brutish and pagan past. We even renamed places, such as Christchurch, to reflect this new belief in the civilising of society through Christianity.

The period before Christ is our pre-history, the prehistoric, a word that implies that no culture existed, or if it did that it was of no consequence. The zeitgeist, as it were, is that we must be a Christian culture, nothing else will do. Yet our pagan culture, and I am talking about the Christchurch area, had an unbroken existence from perhaps 10,000 BC, over 10 times longer than our 1200 years of Christian culture. The pagans were religious in having a set of sophisticated beliefs, if we use Stonehenge as our yardstick. Our Britishness, whatever that means, cannot ignore this legacy. It's that word pagan again. It was, originally, a Latin word meaning villager or rustic before it was hijacked and given its religious significance; to be pagan was to be heathen.

The ancient people of Dorset, as with those in Europe, received a bad press from the Romans. The Gauls, Visigoths and Vandals ultimately sacked Rome, and were lumped together as the barbarian mass. The allusion to barbarian conflicts with the fact that the people in Britannia prospered to such a degree that it merited invasion by the Romans. This shows they were cohesive and organized and it is absurd to call them barbarian. Yes, their technology was hundreds of years behind Rome but the Middle Eastern farming and other metallurgy skills crept, inexorably, through Europe to these isles. Unlike us, with our instant communication, the tribes in Britannia were never aware of this deferred culture, and probably felt that they were at the forefront of farming technology. At least, in recent times, archaeologists and anthropologists have stopped calling these people primitive. They now consider them as sophisticated but hidebound by primitive technology. But what, precisely, is primitive technology?

People in the future will look back to the present time and consider our technology primitive. An illustration of this is the proposal in 2015 to erect wind turbines off the Dorset coast. Whatever their energy merits, these structures would have been visually intrusive. The gerontocracy opposed them on these grounds and ignored the energy need. The solution to this conflict is tidal power, with little visual element and a guaranteed energy supply, yet we do not have the technology to achieve this.

Having considered what the Romans tell us about the Durotriges, I assumed that I could search on the internet and identify a name for the earlier tribe or tribes in Dorset. I found nothing and I decided to invent one. At first, I favoured calling them the Fecundites, from the word fecund, which means fertility, fruitfulness and potency. Then I realized that the word sounded flippant so I played safe, took my cue from the Romans, and settled for the Pre-durotriges.

Finally, we are back to Zuri and her tribe, the Pre-durotriges, in 2200 BC and I need to consider the topography of the area.

Chapter 4

Avonlands

Here I am, at it again, inventing words. We have no name for the region that was nurtured by the River Avon, and Zuri's homeland. It took no time to come up with Avonlands, not a word that I could find anywhere on the internet and I apologize if somebody has used it in the past. I cannot call it the Avon Valley because that name has been adopted by Bristol for its river of the same name. The word Avon is similar to the Welsh word 'Afon' and both mean river. Avon is now a popular unisex child's name.

Avonlands is the homeland, the area that nurtures the first culture, the civilisation even, out of which burst the religious fervour that built Stonehenge. The challenge is to identify the topography and boundary of this region and how it has changed over time.

Stonehenge, rightly, is a World Heritage Site but that is rather like elevating the farm whilst ignoring the fields that grow the crops. Stonehenge was built by a people who were dependent upon the Avon. It was a riverine culture, an entity, a reedy knotted line within which the river gave all life. Stonehenge dominates the middle ground, the heights, just over half way up the river. It is the high place of the Gods and ceremony but the life and the people belong to the river, and the river belongs to Christchurch; the sea end, the focus of communication and trade. Avonlands, the entire area, should be a World Heritage Site and not just Stonehenge.

The Avon is a remarkable river when the archaeology is considered. Each year, more Temples and ancient sites are found along its length, and yet resources to investigate these are sparse. A group of Neolithic Temples found around Damerham, west of Fordingbridge in 2013, is the latest find. In recent years, excavations at the fascinating Marden Henge, near the head of the Avon, have shown this to have been an important ceremonial site. At Marden, 3000 years later, using the Romans as our guide, they commandeered the entire area, with its fertile water meadows, and built a farm and villa on the land. They did that because the land was productive due to the farming started by Zuri's tribe, the Pre-durotriges. An extensive Roman villa was found in April 2016 in Tisbury, Wiltshire. This is situated on the River Nadder, a river that feeds the Avon, and is further evidence of productive land along the Avon catchment. The farming operations since, and the medieval construction of water meadows must have destroyed so much evidence, the remainder now decaying under the mud and silt all down the valley.

The powers that be do not recognize Avonlands. They are content to maintain the usual British fudge, the ad hoc arrangement of counties and county boundaries that make sense over hundreds of years but not millennia. The Pre-durotriges' tribal area has been lost and time has placed Stonehenge in an arbitrary place called Wiltshire. Consequently, its artefacts go to the museum in Salisbury or Devizes. Move a few miles south and Hampshire apprehends the River Avon and any artefacts found, at least in the past, appear to have gone to the museum in Winchester or to storage. Christchurch was moved into Dorset as part of local government reorganisation in 1974 whilst the majority of the River Avon remains in Hampshire.

Artefacts found in Christchurch are sequestered in the Red House Museum in the town, but those found when Christchurch was in Hampshire, are in Winchester. Even Hengistbury Head, an important and integral feature of Avonlands, is now situated in Victorian Bournemouth. Various other artefacts went to museums in South Kensington, who are awarded a huge proportion of government spending on culture, which is unfairly London centric. Meanwhile, English Heritage, entirely indifferent to the counties, to the river, and to Christchurch, and needing the tourist income from Stonehenge, manage it as if it were an exclusive site. People go to Stonehenge and yet see nothing of its hidden landscape, that of the people who created it. Avonlands is no longer the sum of its parts and we need to claim it back to its rightful place.

It is difficult knowing where the tribal boundary existed in Zuri's time because we only have a vague notion of how it was when the Romans arrived. Then, it appears to stretch from the New Forest in the east, Pewsey in the north crossing west over to Warminster and then down to the Devon border at Lyme Regis. None of those names existed at the time, of course. The southern boundary is the coastline, which was further out than now but broadly similar.

Two millennia before the Romans arrived, with a much smaller population, Zuri's people, with no metal ploughs, were restricted to farming the river valleys, but more about that later. Christchurch could readily have been the eastern tribal centre. Imagine it; the earliest hunter-gatherers from Europe in 10,000 BC use the harbour and the lower Avon as their main camp. They prosper and spread upriver to exploit the hunting, often changing camps according to the season. They also spread up the River Stour as far as Stourhead. It is easy to see in studying a modern map how simple it is to leave the Stour, walk east and pick up any valley, follow its watercourse and you must end up on the River Avon. It is a neat river bound triangle of hunting land within which it is difficult to get lost. By 4000 BC the tribe have adopted some farming and so they settle permanently, the population grows and, needing river meadows to farm, they gradually move along each of the subsidiary rivers and streams. Where the river is navigable, they use it as a highway. Otherwise, the river or stream is their walking guide, and the paths follow the watercourses. In the centre of this triangle, the high chalk downs, now called Cranborne Chase, appear to have become an increasingly important ceremonial area. The Chase still harbours a lot of archaeology and much remains to be discovered. This riverine culture needed Gods and religious infrastructure. Stonehenge, high on the chalk downs, was a favoured location. Postholes exist which predate the stone circle and might have been totem poles. Later, they replaced these with a mass of upright tree trunks, in as many as four circles, one inside the other. But in this climate, wood poles rot off quickly so they decide to create more permanent stone circles, and Stonehenge is the most sophisticated example. Zuri's tribe was powerful because Avonlands was the most populated, unified and wealthiest part of Britain. A bounteous, miniscule and yet entire world is created by an arc of chalk hills and the navigable water they discharge to the not so distant sea.

I mull over the footpaths that Zuri might have used and wonder whether modern ordnance survey maps could reflect back that far. In studying the maps, the only dry way out of Christchurch is north, either over or around St Catherine's Hill. The path would then split into two, following either the Stour or Avon. No obvious ancient route survives on the Avon and towards Ringwood modern development and roads overlay the land. Perhaps Zuri crossed to the east bank of the Avon, although there were no bridges or causeways, and the river was deeper in those times. On the east side, the B3347 does appear an ancient line, as it hugs the river. It's also interesting because if it is true that a henge existed where Sopley church sits on its unusual circular churchyard, then we have a Pre-durotriges location. Beyond that, the road flits from farm to farm, each building above the floodplain yet servicing the ancient water meadows. At Ringwood, paths could take both sides of the river but the lanes on the east side look the most ancient. Here, the lanes head north via Rockford and South and North Gorley to Stuckton. It's no surprise that this route leads directly to an Iron Age hillfort called Frankenbury. It's not particularly impressive today but hillforts are always associated with farmland and, sure enough, the water meadows down below are more extensive here. Hillforts were more a retreat than a defensive construction, but maybe this one was also involved with the crossing of the Avon at nearby Fordingbridge. The Allen River joins the Avon at that small town, and up that river is the village of Damerham, where further Neolithic Temples have been identified. The Allen drains land west towards Cranborne Chase and towards the village of Martin, where Zuri was born. It is easy to imagine that as the tribe grew in numbers, the people were forced to inhabit these sheltered river valleys overhung by chalk downs, which were then the point at which the tamed land met the wildwood.

Beyond Fordingbridge, the map gives little away, and paths might have followed both sides of the Avon. Fertile land is abundant along the river, not least at Breamore, but field drainage had not been invented and marshes abounded in those times. When we reach where Salisbury now sits, the Avon has been joined by the rivers Nadder, Wylye, Bourne and Ebble, creating what some refer to as the five rivers. The Avon itself continues up a narrow valley to Amesbury, then passes Durrington Walls on its way to Upavon, where it splits. The western Avon comes in from near Devizes and the Vale of Pewsey, and the spur comes in from near Pewsey itself. The source is 60 miles from Christchurch harbour.

What this all shows is that much more research is necessary to reveal the interaction between the various Neolithic sites and how these were all part of the creation of Stonehenge. A town like Christchurch should be able to promote itself as a part of Avonlands, perhaps the most impressive tribal area in Europe. Christchurch is a key feature in that area, yet one that is unrecognized.

Whenever I am in Christchurch I try to imagine how it was for Zuri, not least as I sup my flat white on the patio of the Fleur de Lys café, sitting opposite Ann. Our bags of M & S goodies sit on the ground beneath the table. The woman on the next table is talking about her financial advisor; it is not a conversation you would hear up North. It is the gerontocracy speaking, and the gerontocracy listening. My thoughts are with Zuri and her Christchurch, because she sat where I now sit, but it was a green promontory then, with views to the sea. I look about and see only the adjacent new apartments for the retired, yet I am aware that the whole town sits over the prehistoric site. We know from past archaeological digs that a mass of artefacts lie under the buildings but much must have been destroyed. It was the same at Hengistbury Head, where hunter-gatherers were evident as early as 10,000 BC. The ironstone that was quarried from the hill in the 1800s destroyed much, and the coastal erosion took away swathes of the land. But I would suggest that the Christchurch promontory, rather more correctly, the peninsula, was more important than Hengistbury. The Neolithic people venerated water long before the Christians adopted it for christening, and appear to have been attracted to high ground bordered by water. Sitting in the Fleur de Lys, the buildings hide the fact that the River Avon and its marsh, and the River Stour and its marsh are less than half a mile apart across the peninsula. The sea marshes cut off the southern end. In the past, these three marshes cut much closer into Christchurch but later buildings and development have pushed them further away and hidden them from view. For Zuri, the only dry way on foot, in and out of the peninsula, was north along the ridge that we now call St Catherine's Hill. Beyond the hill, the Stour and Avon come close together again, and, in effect, make Christchurch very close to an island. The most significant ritual aspect of the peninsula to the Neolithic people is the tip. Coincidentally, this is where Christchurch Priory sits, and I am going to explain later why the pope is so significant as regards this location, that in effect, the pope is Zuri's nemesis.

The Christchurch peninsula is an exceptional geographical

location. If we consider Neolithic trading, it marks the end of two major navigable rivers and looks out over the marshes and the opening to the sea, the major coastal trading route. Experts have suggested that such points might be a node, a point at which trading networks link. It is easy to imagine maritime traders using the location as a focus for their journey. The chartless Neolithic European old salts would advise seagoing traders seeking to go to Avonlands, with the graphic, "Head north, pass between the great white pillars of stone, then swing towards the sunset and behind the hill that looks like a bear's arm." And so The Needles and Old Harry Rocks, of their day, act as the portal into the exceptional natural harbour behind Hengistbury Head. Then, it was newly flooded by rising seas and much smaller than at present, yet it appears no less mythological, no less dramatic, than in those Mediterranean adventures about Jason seeking the Golden Fleece. The Neolithic traders then have a choice between two watery highways heading deep into the hinterlands, where people cluster along the Avon and the Stour. Meanwhile, there is also a considerable fishing and hunting resource in the marshes and sea, food which can be traded inland via the rivers. There was never a town as such on the peninsula preceding Christchurch. The farmers lived in huts, perhaps 500 metres apart, along the margins of the river. They needed to be high enough to avoid the annual floods but close enough to work the water meadows along the river, where they communally farmed. There came a point where this culture reached a peak, which is Zuri's time, when the water meadows were all taken and people had to expand to new land up the tributaries. In the Iron Age, power moved west to the more extensive farmland beneath Maiden Castle and Poundbury Castle around Dorchester. This is why the Romans appear to have relatively ignored the Christchurch area and advanced on West Dorset.

The Roman accounts split the people they found into two groups, the maritime people who lived from the sea and those who lived inland and "do not grow corn but live on milk and flesh and are clad in skins." Whatever, people continued to farm in a similar way, through the Dark Ages, until Christianity arose and a wood church was built in Christchurch, then called Twynham, in AD 800. This was later replaced by the stone Priory. The fact that such a lavish church was built indicates that Christchurch had some significance in those early times, perhaps still based on the farming and fishing developed by Zuri's people. But no major roads passed through the town, principally because of the difficulty crossing the rivers east and west and it was, essentially, a cul de sac approached only from the north, or south from the sea. The natural harbour, fed by two rivers, is the star attraction.

Modern maps did not begin until the 1700s and as late as 1800 the town is very small and comprises of Bargates, through High Street to Bridge Street and Purewell. All the land fronting Bridge Street to Purewell was "liable to floods" as well as the area we now call Quomps. Mudeford was "Muddyford" and Bournemouth was a few buildings recorded as Bourne Heath and Boskom. In Zuri's time, Bournemouth was the great west forest. The great east forest still survives as the New Forest, but it extended further, perhaps 100 miles or more. It is remarkable to appreciate just how little human development existed in and around Christchurch a mere 200 years ago. But smallness and relative obscurity must not be allowed to deny Christchurch its place in history; prehistory that is. Avonlands was a paradise way before the Bible was known, a distinct culture, part of Britannia and yet a world of its own making, a dot on a seaway utilising an unusual, mild, sheltered harbour fed by two rivers. The people prospered and built a Temple, yet understanding why they were here is not the enigma it appears.

Chapter 5

Utility of the Picturesque

I am walking on Hengistbury Head, in bright sunshine, a seascape, a landscape and, not a word in the dictionary, a soundscape. The soft surround sound of waves is punctuated by the tweeting of meadow pipits, birds that come close, not fearing me. In this sensory mood, I realize that Zuri and I are here for entirely different reasons.

At such times, with gorgeous scenery bathed in warm sun, I plunder my brain and rhapsodise on the beauty of England. All that art, poetry and literature wash over me and I am aware that William Gilpin was similarly inspired by our countryside and termed it picturesque. He was the noted vicar at Boldre, Hampshire and interred in the village churchyard in 1804. The picturesque is a scene that is visually pleasing, perhaps vivid. It does not have to be entirely natural and can reflect the hand of man. With Gilpin's insight, I can look across the quarried summit of Hengistbury, to rows of beach huts, moored boats and the engineered coastline and perceive it as attractive, as a fine place to live. This is why the gerontocracy is here and why property prices are so high. The picturesque sustains us intellectually; it is soft and pretty yet without that wildness or remoteness that leaves us feeling intimidated. We also love the romantic, the dreamy world of our poets and our wealth and education allows us the joy of idle reflection. Lord Bute, on his first visit to Highcliffe, was similarly entranced when he thought it the fairest outlook in England.

As for Zuri, with her limited vocabulary, she does not have a word equivalent to picturesque and neither could she conceive of idle musing on fair views. Surely, she would only recognize the utility in the view. That utility would be the advantages offered by the proximity of the coast and the productive land along the river. She knows that from the sea, Hengistbury Head has stature and a distinctive shape, the Hill of the Bear's Arm, which forever marks the harbour entrance and shelters it from the harsh salt wind. To Zuri, the components of this view, such as the Needles off the Isle of White, are mere columns of white chalk that identify precisely where she is; that is their utility.

I pursue the local picturesque by walking in Zuri's footsteps up St Catherine's Hill whilst pondering over how her experience and mine vary over 4000 years. Today, the summit trig point, near the shooting range, is just 45 metres above sea level and a number of tumuli (burial mounds) and other earthworks are situated along the hill. These did not appear for perhaps 1000 years after Zuri died. Neither do we know whether the hill was covered in trees in her time, or whether the tribe had felled them for firewood and building their huts. On my path a massy sky hung over a low east horizon, the skyline formed by the New Forest. The trees create an even line with few identifiable features. Zuri's family would have headed out into a similar pathless wilderness to hunt deer and boar. Below, the silver Avon forms a sinuous loop in the valley, the water meadows laid out to the south, and unendingly to the north, where they blend into further countless trees. The Needles lie, hazily, on the southern horizon, and Hengistbury Head, at just 36 metres high, dominates to the right. The sea is a thin sliver of blue and the harbour just shows around the marsh, backed, rather obviously, by the beach huts on the sand spit. It is an amazing synthesis of seemingly unspoiled land, sea and sky, a scene of great beauty.

Christchurch itself is cosily settled, dimpled as it were, into the trees, with the Priory proud and upstanding over a chequerboard of roof tiles. Elsewhere, there are a few isolated buildings but little spoils this essentially pastoral view, not even roads. It is amazing to consider that it looks much the same today as it must have looked in 2200 BC. It is a similar view to that which Zuri saw, when she farmed the valley. To her it was not beautiful, rather more a green scene of abundance and security. She did not have to ignore the noise and the stress induced by traffic and the fact that it is difficult to find quiet and calm places here, in our time. I would have described the view west, over the River Stour, but mature pines line that side of the hill and obscure the vista.

In pursuit of utility and the reason why Zuri's tribe did so well here, I decided to study the soils. It was June when I walked over the Avon water meadows from Christchurch. The walk had an inauspicious start because I stopped to talk to a salmon fisherman. He decried the collapse in salmon running the river, a run that starts in March and peaks in June and July. Not only were there fewer salmon but nobody caught the big fish, in excess of forty pounds, that were here as recently as the 1950s. I decided not to tell him that before Zuri's time, huge salmon were so massed in the water that they were flicked out by brown bear claws. The bears caught so many that they only ate the principal muscles and tossed the remainder to the ground, where eagles, vultures and gulls fought over them.

Further upriver I moved out into the damp meadows where wildflowers and orchids appeared together with spotted burnet moths and, in the river, yellow water-lily, called the brandy bottle, in amongst masses of water reed. The cattle in the fields, as if it was still Zuri's time, knew that the reeds were edible, even delicious. Leaning over the embankment steel shuttering they had eaten a trough into the vegetation along the bank equal to the length of their necks. Underfoot, the ground undulated, higher meant drier and lower meant wetter, even to water pooling in places. Yet height is relative and a concrete trig point beside the path records a height of just three metres above sea level on the OS map. The cattle had disturbed the ground in many places and removed all vegetation and I had what I had hoped for; exposed soil.

The topic of orgasmic pleasure is rather limited in this book, as it is generally with gerontocratic life, and few modern people would associate soil with arousal. But I started work as a gardener and became an organic vegetable grower after I retired. I pushed 30 barrows of compost to my vegetable patch each winter, a musty, living mulch laid over the soil, a form of foreplay, a caress that promised a certain ecstasy at some point. The ecstasy was that first warm spring day when I suddenly found myself fondling the moist, dark, crumbly soil, running it through my hands, a soil bursting with fecundity, the rich black soil of ancient dreams. I will avoid an analysis of the various erotic pleasures of life, but suffice to say that a good soil makes the earth move for me; like no other.

Zuri will have felt this, for all those who rely on the soil feel this. And here it was, under my feet, the Christchurch water meadow. I take care not to excessively romanticize the water meadow; it's a food factory, a place of crops and fodder, a place where people drowned, were injured or just dropped down due to exhaustion. Also, they were working with inefficient antler and bone tools. It must have been a place of despair, as with no weather forecasts, they will have planted seed and then watched it wash out, their future floating away on the floodwater.

I decided to look at the Stour water meadows and started at Iford Bridge, walking up the Stour Valley Way; it was not a good experience. The riverbank was covered in litter, the waste bins overflowing onto the path, and the dog poo bin was stinking and covered in flies. There also seemed very little bird life on the river and the water had a blackish look. A little research showed that at least ten conurbations discharge treated sewage into the Stour. We can add in septic tanks and the phosphate from farmland and the ever increasing abstraction of water for new housing. That is the Stour. In this state it is not technically defined as polluted and is classified as stressed. Zuri experienced none of this and in her day the Stour and the Avon had a cleaner and greater flow than today. The rivers, the lifeblood of Christchurch in Zuri's time, now import other people's waste. But, focussing on the trees, the reeds and the sunlight, the river at least appeared attractive. I crossed the footbridge over the A338 and the vehicle noise became stressful. I realized that Holdenhurst, an attractive village, had been destroyed by the building of that road, but at least I could see the water meadows, much smaller than on the Avon side of Christchurch, but used by Zuri's people for farming. The irony was that this walk was undoubtedly safer in her day, as I dodged cars driving far too fast on the lane. I gave up, walked back to Christchurch and considered the soils on the far side of the Avon where I live. I realized that even if Zuri's people could readily cross the river, either wading or by boat, the soils on the Friars Cliff and Highcliffe side are mere stony heath, lacking the fertility for farming and always very dry. Even the hinterland, the land around Burton and Bockhampton, drained by the River Mude, is similarly poor. That said, these poor soils, because they do not suit the strong growing and ultimately stifling grass species, are ideal for the mass of herbs, the wild plants, that Zuri seeks. They are also ideal for a wide range of fungi, another valuable food source. Poor soil matters little today, when the soil is purely a medium, and irrelevant providing enough oil based fertilizer is applied. The fact is, Zuri's community could only have prospered up to the point at which the available, and very limited, fertile land along the river could be farmed.

Zuri would understand the utility of the soil, a subject lost to us now. I find it amazing that we, the gerontocracy, buy a property, pay masses of attention to the interior yet rarely assess the soil in the garden. We don't care whether it is fertile or otherwise because we have the money to put that right. We can ship in soil or add compost or fertilizer simply because our wealth shields us from the reality of the natural world. Well, at least we think it does.

Zuri was born near the present village of Martin, near the head of the Allen River, above Fordingbridge. Her family were hunter- gatherers, some of the last. They hunted the wildwood of Cranborne Chase and traded skins with farmers. They lived on chalk soil and Zuri knew the difference between this poor medium and the fertile soils along the streams and rivers. Farming will expand up her valley in the future and cause the degradation of the land due to over-cropping, over-grazing and the felling of the trees. Perhaps she experienced some of that whilst she was alive. The farming Gods of Stonehenge meant nothing to the hunter-gatherers like Zuri's family, whose ancient Gods did not live in wood or stone circles. I am also mindful that other hunter-gatherer groups might have existed down in Christchurch, those who lived purely on the marine environment. Although we know that farming will come to dominate, nothing is known about how these cultures coexisted barring a smidgeon of information arising from German excavations. There, the hunter-gatherers and farmers lived side by side for some time, and interbreeding took place between the two groups, but with conditions. It seems that women from hunter-gatherer groups were taken into the farming group, but it was not acceptable for any of the farming people to do the reverse. We can sense, even at this distance, how status is creeping in. The farmer, perhaps the cattle farmer, dominates society.

Although it must have been traumatic for Zuri to move down the river and "marry", it had its consolations. There, she meets people travelling up and down the river, the principal highway. She listens to coastal traders and hears stories about the area we call Europe, not that she knew where or what that was. I can hardly call Zuri cosmopolitan but it is evident to us now that those ancient societies that traded were also the most innovative and possessed a wider vocabulary. The Pre-durotriges were not isolated, or ignorant. In fact, the gerontocracy and the Pre-durotriges have so much in common. The gerontocracy has a high incidence of contact with London and they travel all over the world and have financial skills. When you casually talk to an old person in Christchurch then you need to take care. The depth of knowledge, or experience behind that wrinkly face can take you by surprise and references to engineering, aviation or finance can be anticipated. Second homes or a luxury boat on a river have a habit of leaping into the conversation. The gerontocracy has a wide vocabulary and status is paramount. This is not the case when I return to rural Shropshire, where London is despised, the professions rare and boats on the river usually refer to a coracle used by ever rarer salmon fishermen.

The picturesque river dominates our shopping trips into Christchurch, and the walk along Bridge Street, with pretty bridges, has a processional feel, as if the engineer who built it felt pleased to have somehow tamed the River Avon. Perhaps it is a superficial belief, reliant on fair weather and outdated data about annual rainfall and averages. Global warming has upset the average and we have yet to catch up. Ann and I cross the first bridge onto the island, and then off the island onto the peninsular, by the castle. The murky water creates conflict, as the picture postcard view counterbalances the flood threatening monster, something that modern technology and unlimited resources thought it could tame. The floods up North were said to be a one in one hundred years phenomena, yet they happen again and again. Ann and I look at the waterside buildings on this walk and we are agreed never to buy a property near the river. Yet, to Zuri, the flood brought silt and was the giver of life much like the Nile is to Egypt. The flood was a utility, a benefit to the people and not something to fear.

I need a haircut and the hairdresser's shop is situated beyond the Norman keep, that edifice built a mere blip back into the past by other European invaders. The river once lapped the keep walls, a living moat, but is now held back by the sward of a bowling green and the bowlers of the gerontocracy. The green sward is mere centimetres above potential inundation, the consequence of too many houses and too much development impeding the water meadows, nature's flood management. My hairdresser spends more time finding my hairs than cutting them, and during the search she explained how she grew much of her own food and did I know that the nutrient levels of modern food was so low. They use too much water and fertilizer, she informed me. It shocked me that in the proletariat, people know so much and yet are ignored. The politicians ignore everybody; they don't listen. The contrast with Zuri zipped into my mind; she is listened to, she plays her part in communal life because she has the knowledge, she finds food. Zuri is, in herself, a utility. She receives immediate feedback and feels valued. Zuri's immediacy contrasts with our feelings of impotency and frustration, our inability to change or influence anything, and so we, the gerontocracy, spoil by voting for Brexit, the young despair of us.

Oh, I don't know, perhaps I have it all wrong. I call out, "Ann, the sun's shining; let's walk down to Avon Beach for a coffee." I feel a need to gaze out to sea and think about Neolithic food.

Chapter 6

The Food Factory

Should eating, in 2017, be this complicated? I need to reduce my salt intake so I study every item of food I buy, particularly those I am not familiar with, to ascertain its sodium content. Then I have to multiply the sodium by two and a half times to measure the actual salt, and on this occasion I've also forgotten my damned glasses. Why is the text so small? Why is sodium written in the contents and not salt? No wonder people get irritated; I am a cretinous mathematician dietician hypertensive, but only if I eat certain treats. And those salty treats include cakes and biscuits; egg custards and digestives are the worst. Why do they use so much salt in confectionary?

An elderly woman backed into me, her elbow digging into my side, another woman clipped my heel; others step in front of me to reach a portion of Icelandic cod, demonstrating their annoyance at my prevarication over what to buy. The gerontocracy has a problem with spatial awareness, of judging distance, and they can be so damned impatient. Perhaps with death so close, the next minute appears very precious? With death in mind, I am already in heaven, gerontocracy heaven; M & S on Christchurch High Street. They display all those treats that make this life so enjoyable. With great deliberation, I select some strawberry tarts, any unusual fish dishes, and some specialist tea. The "lemon, ginger and ginseng" is my favourite; its caffeine free but, at my age, the ginseng content makes me anxious. Ann brought me back to reality when she said "Isn't it wonderful that we can buy whatever food we want." Is this the mantra of the gerontocracy?

It would be a mistake to think that Zuri had a limited and nutrient poor diet compared to ours. She can choose from sturgeon steaks, caviar, salmon, brown trout, beaver, venison, seal steaks, roast boar, roast bear, roast aurochs, a myriad of shellfish, lobster, cod, geese, swan, bustard, grain and a vast array of green plants and fungi; perhaps even meadowsweet ale. By 2017, the sturgeon, aurochs, beaver and bear have long since gone, the seal and shellfish are struggling, a few lightweight salmon are caught but then we have to put them back into the river. Our salmon now come from Scottish fish farms. The bustard has been reintroduced on Salisbury Plain but is off the menu. The swans abound but only because they dropped off the menu after the gluttony of the Tudors. I recognize that I have to take care when assessing Zuri's diet, what she habitually ate. As an omnivore, she is opportunistic and can eat a vast range of foods because she has a sophisticated digestive system, which in itself consumes much energy. At times of famine she had the ability to eat food that was probably not habitually part of their diet. But many of the plants around today were not known to her. As I walk from Riversmeet to Stanpit in Christchurch, the path is lined by the bulky green mass of alexanders, a common plant that looks like overgrown celery. All parts can be eaten, including the root but research shows it to have been introduced by a Roman gastronome who knew that it would like the damp soils of the Avon water meadows. Zuri could not have known it or many of the plants we are familiar with today.

The water meadow is a silt soil, laid over thousands of years by floods and nutrified annually by the inundation. Such meadows now form a tiny constituent of the 7% of world soils that can actually be classified as fertile. One third of all the arable soil in the world has been lost since Zuri's time. The soil in water meadows sits just above the water table and any plant growing in it has the perfect medium, with its head in the sun and its roots in moisture. But there is far more to it than that, as Zuri knew. She lived in a time without metal and without a beast of burden, so if people are to grow crops then all tilling involved human toil. They were aware that they could not till heavy soils like clay but they were not impotent and could impeach the Gods for favour. The Gods gave them light soils that were nutrient rich, well watered and yet tillable by hand, the soils of the Christchurch water meadows, where the Avon and Stour rivers did much of the hard labour for them. Although I use the term water meadow, the single word watermeadow(s) appears on OS maps and may reflect medieval agriculture, when they created channels to irrigate land alongside the river. Zuri would know them as natural flood meadows and, as far as we know, her people were not aware of irrigation techniques. What she did know was that a light tilling of the soil was needed to sow Emmer wheat (Triticum dicoccum) and Einkorn wheat (Triticum monococcum) and it grew tall and sturdy, as well as barley (probably Hordeum vulgare). As evidence of this, Emmer Wheat was found in Wiltshire and dated to 4064 – 3640 BC. When I walked the Avon water meadows, I looked up at St Catherine's Hill, aware that the entire hill is poor soil, mostly gravel and sand, too poor for farming and without water for cattle. On the Scottish border they would have called such areas The Waste. The land is similar on the chalk downs further up the river, with its poor fertility and dryness.

Research suggests that women like Zuri, who gathered plants, became expert on local soils because they knew which plants needed fertile land and which grew in other mediums. But there was only enough fertile soil in and around Christchurch and Avonlands for a limited population. That is why, ultimately, all the power shifted, by the Iron Age, to the rich clay soils of the Thames Valley and East Anglia. Recent archaeology in East Anglia has found huge fish traps, and the archaeologist involved said that it was evidence of a population move from the Stonehenge area to the East coast.

My research on how Zuri's tribe farmed in Christchurch kept throwing up the word horticulturalist, so I read my first book on anthropology to understand what is meant by the word. This indicated that horticulture was an early term for agriculture. As a gardener myself, I then understood that my training in the early 1960s was essentially Victorian and is little understood or of use today. The Gardener's Bible was his jobbing diary, which he, as there were few women gardeners, consulted at the start of each working day. Summer bedding plants were never planted before the seventh of June to avoid late frost, and seeds were sown on time honoured dates. These gardeners, as with Zuri, spent their life dominated by the seasons. The relationship between longer daylight hours and the harvesting of plants would also have become a sixth sense. The year closed when fungi appeared and the hours of light shortened but the precise dates, such as the summer solstice, surely that was a problem before diaries were invented.

At first, I assumed Zuri's tribe would use the moon, the synodic cycle, as it is known. It is quite simple because the new moon starts the month, assuming that you can see it. In cloudy Britannia that is a real issue. Even today, some gardeners swear by lunar planting and suggest that various plants only flourish dependent upon the phase of the moon at the time of planting. But just counting the new or full moons to know roughly where you are in the year is not quite so simple. The moon moves on an ellipse, at times closer to earth and larger, and otherwise further away and smaller. So a lunation, a single cycle, is 29.5 days. To avoid the half day, one counts 29 days one month, and 30 the next. But that leaves the year at least 11 days short and some years have 13 new moons. The moon and solar cycles are also incommensurable and do not work together. That said, Saudi Arabia and the Islamic faith use the synodic cycle in arranging the Hajj. That means it takes place 12 days earlier each year, and only occurs at the same time every 33 years.

Knowing the moon's cycle has little meaning to us today, other than for tide tables, as we shut ourselves away in houses each night. But, our eyes are far more adapted to moonlight than we realize. The peripheral part of our retina contains rods, which help us to see in poor light. It takes perhaps 40 minutes for the eyes to adapt to poor light, but we switch off this facility when we switch on an electric light. Zuri, with only fire as a light source, and constant use of her rods, will have had a much faster and better ability to use moonlight, and to know when the full moon was out, even under cloud. They would believe in the superlunar, that something significant, what we might call spiritual, is associated with the moon.

Zuri's people may have used the synodic cycle albeit with annual solar corrections. They ritualized the shortest and longest days each year at Stonehenge and, unlike Islam, needed fairly precise dates. This is easily achieved by measuring shadows using upright wood posts and this may be why totem poles or wood circles were in use before Stonehenge was built. The shaman at Stonehenge or the earlier wood circles would calculate when the sun approached its zenith and then set a day for the ceremony. Yet they still needed to set dates for planting grain and other crops, as too early holds the danger of frosts and too late shortens the period to harvesting. Perhaps they celebrated the summer solstice and then counted moons to harvest time.

Zuri's time is sometimes called the birth of civilisation, and the move to horticulture and early farming appears to have occurred relatively quickly and successfully. It was probably after a long period of development that the various farming skills ultimately came together and created a surplus or at least a continuity of food which powered the building of Stonehenge. Because farming then relied on human labour the grain from farming would not have been sufficient to create a carbohydrate diet over a full year. We know they stored the grain and it was probably seen as a winter and spring food supply, a fall-back in those sparse times. The more grain that remained uneaten the more seed corn they had available for the next harvest.

To Zuri, Avonlands was a mass of food sources. We, the

gerontocracy and aloof from nature, do not realize how rare such locations are in the world, as we open another pack of fertilizer and unravel the hosepipe. Anthropological studies suggest that it is very rare for any hunter-gatherer tribe to create a surplus, and perhaps the only proven case is the Potlatch Indians of the North Pacific coast. They had an excess of food because they lived on productive, navigable waterways and had access to coastal fish stocks and rich hunting in forests, although they never farmed. As a means of displaying status, they actually wasted food in front of guests, simply because they could. Similar displays of excess by Zuri's people occurred at Durrington Walls where meat was buried uneaten. Avonlands offered a similar environment to that which the Potlatch experienced with the addition of milder winters and fertile land along the river.

If I seek evidence of an excess of food in the Neolithic then it is pretty thin on the ground, not least because we have ruined the wildness in Avonlands. It does not help that the archaeology tends to seek sites of occupation, and not evidence of the more esoteric farming or hunting skills. But granaries were found at an Iron Age site at Britford, just south of Salisbury, that stored Emmer or Einkorn wheat. Wheat was also found beneath the sea at Bouldner Cliff, Isle of Wight and dated to 6000 BC but this is suggested to be an import from Europe. As regards freshwater fish as food, the Avon is considered to have more variety of fish than any other river in the Britain. I could not find a reason for this.

I muse on Zuri's food as we call at a German supermarket to stock up for the week. I include some Château Lafitte Lidl. Perhaps the German owners are aware that the gerontocracy does not shop at their store because, unlike M & S, they provide poor labelling, with little or no information on ingredients like salt. We shop carefully, valuing food and rarely throw any away. We choose organic where possible and British, and, like Zuri, food that makes the gut work. I should correct that statement as

Zuri did not understand what made the gut work, but she could hardly avoid lots of roughage.

Experts suggest that prehistoric people ate as many as 700 different plants and animals each year, strictly in seasonal order. Some people now pursue this as the Paleo diet because, according to the latest research, it ideally suits our gut, a veritable food factory, which thrives on variation, a wide range of mainly green foods, fruit, vegetables and meat. The grains and dairy diet began during Zuri's time and some experts see this as detrimental to our health. Alternative eating, fads you might say, like the DASH and SIRT diets, push us away from sugar, fats and processed food and over to curly kale, spinach and other leafy eating. These natural foods suit our gut flora, the microbiome of 100 trillion microbes and over 1000 species, which maintain our immune system and supply many nutrients. It is no surprise that scientists now consider hazelnuts, Zuri's favourite food, as perfect for the microbiome. The microbes don't appear to thrive on takeaways or pasta, food that is little more than excess calories. There are apparently 70,000 edible plants in the world yet we now tend to survive overwhelmingly on just three, those of rice, wheat and corn. Our microbiome needs diverse natural food to flourish and the wider the range the more healthy it becomes. Also, Zuri's microbiome, without our antiseptic hand washing and sterilisation, will have been much richer. Neither could she avoid exchanging microbes with the animals and fish she ate, as well as all those unwashed plants and roots.

The microbiome resembles an internal compost heap. Similar to a heap of compost in the garden, the mix of ingredients is fundamental to how well it works. Heat, oxygen and moisture are essential and rather like compost, the heap is easily put out of kilter. Too much stodge is similar to too much fresh grass and suffocates the microbes. When that happens to the microbiome it is now known that you cannot be healthy and well. What poisons the gut microbes may come as a shock. Let's start with antibiotics, especially when given to children, and how about chlorine in our water, and emulsifiers, and artificial sweeteners, several reasons why the latest science suggests we might not thrive. The irony of course is that no gardener would dream of putting such products on their compost heap, yet we swallow them with impunity.

Zuri and I received our gut flora from our mother, a mouthful of gubbins as we slid down the birth canal. An increasing number of births are now by caesarean section and the baby loses this advantage. As a member of the gerontocracy, it also appears that I have a healthy gut because my mother and I were fed clean basic food and water before the 1960s and experienced less chemicals and additives. Perhaps that is why we also have the least allergies.

Zuri's people took a communal approach and unwritten rules would have divided the water meadows and the marsh between the family groups, to prevent dispute over who took what. The crops, the periodic surpluses, would have been shared and we can add the seasonal salmon run up the river, the sloe berries, the blackberries, the crab apples and the mass of hazelnuts in autumn. She must have realized that hazelnuts gave her energy yet could not know, as we do, that they provided 628 calories per 100 grams. A similar amount of watercress offered a meagre 11 calories. With so few sugary foods she does not know fatness or obesity and yet, like the bears, she understands the need to eat well, to stock up, as we used to say, before running into winter. And eat well they did, in variety if not in consistent quantity, adding spit roasted pigs, beef, grain and dairy to their foraged food. The evidence shows that large pots were used for meat casseroles and smaller pots for dairy, which also seemed to have had a ritual purpose. Perhaps the white milk was a magical substance, like chalk. The LeCHE project is researching why we Europeans, particularly the British, are lactose tolerant beyond the age of 7 or 8 years. The majority of adult people in the world cannot digest milk, and this advantage is said to have given us 19% more fertile offspring.

There is a suggestion here that farming and living on their own produce, from milk to beef and grain, was an aspiration. The consumption of beef might have made the herby, green diet of the plebs, lose its allure. The fact that an excess of meat and fat are bad for the gut has only recently been highlighted. It would be easy to see this as the familiar battle between the vegetarian and the meat eater but for Zuri it also influenced the battle of the sexes. As beef and dairy expanded, which was male work, the female forager role, Zuri's role, was relegated to that of support rather than mainstay. Each of the sexes had a defined role to play and one was becoming subsidiary to the other.

The seasonal work load on Zuri and her family must have been intense, especially when cultivating, sowing and harvesting. A man or woman's labour, as any vegetable grower knows, hardly covers the energy expended in that effort and there is little surplus. Both male and female skeletons from that period show enormous wear and tear on joints, not least the spine. Iron plough shares might reduce this, but not for a 1000 years. And the iron plough, pulled by oxen, was also men's work, and would empower them to the further disadvantage of women.

Even though farming is increasing, the hunting of deer and perhaps other animals is still pursued in the forests. We can assume that the deer were food but it may be that the need for antlers and bone was the principal reason to hunt. They dug pitfall traps, two metres deep, overlain with alder stakes and probably set cord or rope snares. When they caught the deer the skin was carefully removed so that it could be used for clothing or trade. It was usual to abandon the animal pelvis and spine on site, this being too heavy, and carry only the useable meat, marrow bones, tendons, skin and antlers back to the hut. At the kill they would remove the stomach first with the intestines attached, empty these and then use them to collect the blood as they butchered the animal. Strong odours and irritating flies would be a daily experience. Back at the huts, the meat and offal would be divided amongst the people, as well as the skin and tendons. The meat would go into a big pot, braised in water with added plants and roots. We now realize that by cooking this way the fluid and greens reduced the carcinogen levels in the meat. This pot boiled food was then available for all family members no matter what time they arrived. They are thought to have eaten twice a day. At some stage they would agree their various tasks, not least to address the seasonal plants or roots they expected to find. The children would manage the few cattle, which were wilder and smaller than modern cattle. They had to keep them away from the crops and perhaps herd them up onto St Catherine's Hill to browse on trees and shrubs, more like goats than modern cattle that eat only grass. Experts would argue that because dairy cattle can produce calves for ten years, much of their herd would be lactating. These cows would need twice the amount of water as beef cattle and had to return frequently down to the river to drink. The older children would carry a flint axe and cut light branches off particular species of trees to supplement the cattle diet. Few family members would be in a position to return to the hut for what we term lunch. The various herbs, plants and fungi, would be added to the pot as they were found, plus fish or shellfish, so that the content was constantly replenished. They will have used the bones, meat and fat, and the braising would have broken down the collagen, the connective tissue, into gelatine no matter what the age of the deer or cattle.

The sun is not consistent enough in Britain to dry fish or meat and this limits Zuri's ability to store food. The plant food would need to be collected daily and eaten relatively quickly, from plot to plate, as we now say. I doubt they understood that this retained the maximum amount of nutrient in the food.

Bones were a useful storage device as they protect the nutritious marrow, which would not need to be eaten immediately. They could have roasted them in order to melt the marrow and then store it as a kind of butter. Otherwise, they could readily retain the bones, perhaps as a fallback food store, and crack them open on cold winter nights, to eat marrow rather than hazelnuts.

Like so many people throughout the world, even today, Zuri thinks that the Gods will provide her with food no matter what. She kills without compunction, albeit with an oblation, perhaps just a gesture of gratitude to the Gods for the provender. She goes on killing even though the game is more difficult to find. Her people drove to extinction, the aurochs, the wolves, the bears, the beaver, the seals, the sturgeon, and a myriad of other animals and birds; this was justified by her Gods. These beliefs meant that her people thrived because they had a right to exploit all other living things, to take more than their fair share. This is no different to the Christian faith which gave us dominion over the land and its creatures. It is an imbalance, as one side transfers life to a burgeoning other, but it is not sustainable. As the Neolithic population increased all but people were diminished and it changed forever this area I call Avonlands. It is a notion that makes me look with scepticism at those television programmes featuring North American Indian and similar tribes, all decrying modern life and claiming to be the guardians of the environment, a spurious claim. Yes, they lived close to nature but it was a killing embrace, where nature only survives if human numbers remain low. The irony is that we now consider the denuded chalk downs, stripped of their ancient forest, as picturesque, and we do not miss the aurochs and wildlife that relied upon the trees. That pretty patchwork of hedged fields up the River Avon, a human manufacture, is also picturesque and the farmer is promoted as the guardian of the English countryside. Any mention of re-wilding the land, allowing some to return back to how it was before people changed it, is treated with derision. None of the wildness remains; Zuri's people began that destruction.

I am aware that it is easy for me, as a member of the gerontocracy, to cast aspersions. It does not help that I am in the pub in Portesham, near Dorchester, eating a delicious Shilvinghampton beef casserole for dinner; I employ other people to do my killing. In fairness I am hungry. I had spent the day on the South Dorset Ridgeway researching the wealth of burial chambers and stone circles on that fascinating eerie spot. Zuri's tribal power moved east to the Dorchester area because there was nowhere to expand in Avonlands. They moved because they could exploit the extensive farmland, and here I am, 4000 years later, paying big money for grass fed beef grown on the prehistoric grasslands of Dorset. This is how I spend my days but how did Zuri spend her days in Christchurch, on the ground where the M & S store now sits?

Chapter 7

A Day in the Life of…

After the third moon, she watched and she waited. The peewit's union, their coming together, she had noted at each sun and she knew the nest sites in the bay. The birds, full of mating fever, flew whirling, looping circles in the air and called to each other but were careless and gave their nests away; Zuri needed the eggs. The gulls, with the eye of the eagle, also watched and took all eggs, any eggs, and they searched before the sun could be seen, silent white spirits in the half light.

There was a light chill breeze blowing from the north and it flattened and calmed the water as the tide ebbed. Zuri knew her presence would keep the gulls away and give her first take. Everyone knew that this was her area to forage and they stayed away; the gulls did not care. She would take the first clutch but leave the second to grow and to fly; they would return at the next breeding time. The peewits did not understand that they were a gift to Zuri from the Gods. She, for her part, must care for them by trapping the wolves, foxes, stoats and weasels. That was the pact, the first clutch to pay for the bird's safekeeping in the marsh.

She felt wet and chill, being covered in mud and sand after wading between the slacks and islands. She knew that it was too early to tread on the foot stinging fish, as they came with the high sun. If she trod on one it swelled the foot with much pain so she shuffled her feet through the sand, to dislodge the fish and make them swim away. It was a habit they all developed when walking in soft sand.

Although she knew where most of the birds were, finding the nest was another matter. The nest and the eggs were part of the earth; they did not want to be found and acted with plants and pebbles in order to deceive her, or was it to cheat the gulls? She knew that if the Gods were with her, the bird would sit motionless until almost trodden upon and would then fly and show itself. Even then, the meagre nest, a mere dimple in the pebbles, gave nothing away and a careful search was still required. Sometimes, the birds flew up before she reached them and then mobbed her, coming close to her head and sometimes striking her hair. When she found the eggs, she placed them in her basket and made a supplication to Cofu, thanking the God for his gift. She always appeased the God, who gave the bird's flight and the power to disappear until the next nesting time.

As the sun rose she found four nests, each with four eggs, and knew that it was all she would find. Looking around the bay she could see other foragers, mostly women and probably egg seekers. She walked with care, knowing a fall or getting into deep water might see her lose or crack the eggs. She finally reached dry land and followed it along the river's edge. Here, sea carrot was sending up its first leaves, feathery, bright and green. Zuri picked many handfuls, carefully removed the eggs and repacked them in the leaves. She knew this plant, that if picked young and fresh the leaves would quickly regrow and provide food for many suns but turn bitter when the flowers showed. Then, she would bring her digging stick to remove some roots for eating and, as with the eggs, leave some for the next season. Nearby was some garlic mustard, now just a bundle of young leaves, unrecognisable to others without its flower but she knew it and placed handfuls in her bag. Then, along the river and clear of the bay, she put the skin bag safely on the ground. Aware that her arms and legs glistened with drying salt, she stepped into the fresh water and washed the white away. She continued towards the hut and wondered how the matriarch would use the eggs. Sometimes they were added to the stock pot but she preferred them cooked separately. The cooking depended on what food the others collected and it was the time of the waxing sun, and everywhere the joy of soft, fresh growth. The creatures too, were occupied with the warming sun but mating made them careless and she and the family would eat well.

The eggs and leaves safely delivered, Zuri walked back down the river and around the headland to where the yellow gorse blossomed. The bees were buzzing all over the flowers, attracted by its sweet scent. This reminded her of the honey they stole when they found the nests of bees. Avoiding the sharp spines, she plucked the yellow flowers and ate them as she walked. It was when the shore turned yellow with gorse that the horsetail cones would spring out of the ground. She knew where they were and could collect the emerging plant tips just once, otherwise the plant died. The shamaness would use them to make potions for when the women had water problems, which the men never had. The women laughed when they picked the horsetail cones because they looked short and stubby, just like the men's zakila, through which they passed their pee. The horsetail cones had to be picked and taken to the shamaness immediately, as they quickly went limp and lost their freshness. She returned to the hut and carried a beaver pelt and a small bowl outside, where she sat down in the light. The handling of the pelt immediately released its rancid odour, the smell of stale fat. She smeared some of the bowl contents, a creamy mixture of deer brain and pee, inside the pelt and began scraping with a piece of flint. The odour of the mixture had a peculiar smell. Who decided that it should be men's pee to be used in the mix? Why was it better than from a woman?

Zuri was proud of her skill in preparing pelts. It was not easy, scraping and smearing, so that the skin did not get too dry or too thin. If this happened then the hair fell out and the pelt was not wanted by traders. She knew that beaver pelts were becoming rare and there was a high demand for them, so she took much care. The skin on the inside needed to be smooth and supple and without odour. She did not have to take such care when working with course cattle skins, the ones that kept them warm at nights.

As she scraped, the children hustled the cattle past the hut on their way down to the river to drink. The splat of their droppings reminded her of how much they needed milk and meat, the food that made them secure. The splats resounded across the calm quiet of the valley. When the cowpats had dried, the children would collect the crusts and take them down to the water meadow to go onto the soil. She called out to the children, saying did they want their skin scraping, and they all laughed. She looked at the cattle, easy in the warmth and their tails lashing; all but one of the cows had a calf beside them. She knew the cows would go directly to the river without hesitating, and they did, thirsty for water to replace the milk the calf was taking. The one without a calf was their milch cow. With its flaccid udders it was not in need of milking. Its calf had died and as they needed a milch cow, it meant that they did not have to kill a calf in the usual way. They had missed that succulent meat, as they would not eat a calf that had died, a calf that the Gods had taken.

The bull followed the cows and walked into the water but did not drink, wary, eying his unions and calves, and sometimes snorting. The bull's need to garner, to hold his little group together, had always stirred Zuri. If you separated him from the cows or stood in his way, then his blood heated and he turned fierce and could run at you. His need to protect touched her; she felt both fearful and at one with him and it was because she was with child. That gave her both joy and anxiety. The blood had not appeared for some moons and she sensed changes in her body, the same changes that the other women had talked about; she had listened intently but she gave nothing away. She knew that as soon as she was known to be with child her role would change. Those with child stayed around the hut and were sheltered from hard foraging but she knew that this meant scraping skins sun in, sun out. So she made mute words to the Gods, thankful to be with child yet craving their protection; that the Gods had to take the part of the bull and watch over her. She was here on the river because so many women died when they were with child. This thought stopped her scraping and she put her hand to her boar's tooth amulet.

Zuri returned to scraping and massaging the pelt. The matriarch moved about, often a cooking pot or bowl in her hands, adding this or that, and returning to the fire in the hut. Zuri was aware that the matriarch would feed the shaman and shamaness that sun, as they and the other families took their turn to feed them. The matriarch would demand the choicest food and if there had been a kill, the best parts of the beast would be for the shaman and shamaness. They accepted the food and in return performed rituals that gave joy to them all and kept the Gods watching over them. The shaman frightened Zuri. He was a small man, with animal in him, and walked as if he was a fox and through the fox he knew everything about animals. He told stories about the animals and how people only survived because of them, the gift of the Gods. The shamaness would be with him and she knew the cures and incantations which would bring them through childbirth and illness. Whenever they were uneasy or anxious they called on her and she always knew what to do or what to take.

The matriarch took one of the smaller children to the granary pit. The lid was lifted and the child climbed in to scoop up some grain. There was little left after the dark times but with the rising sun, they would manage until the high sun and the harvest. Zuri stopped scraping, sat back and looked out over the river. Many generations ago, a forebear had chosen this spot because it commanded a view of the river and all the approaches. From here, they never missed movement in the water and would even know if it were a fish or a seal. They did not see many seals now but to kill one was a great gift of food, oil and skin. They could also see people, those who paddled up and down the river, traders with bundles in the boat, probably furs, or fisherman with a catch of silver shiny fish. Beyond, into the marsh she could see the reeds they would cut at the high sun for roofing huts and as fodder if the grass went dry. She could hear the warbling of the small birds that flitted through the reeds, as if the whole world was raising kin.

She felt uncomfortable and moved her position. A nodule of skin on the fur impeded her scraping so she selected another small piece of flint and carefully sliced it away. She had to take care because the traders would look over every part of the skin and then quibble about any cuts or flaws. The fur side of the pelt was slinky and would not stay still as she worked. She hung the skin high up in the hut, where it would be dry and away from the dogs. A wet skin would rot and smell.

The matriarch brought her a bowl filled with stew from the cooking pot. The bowl was a rounded stump that had been selected to sit neatly into a hand, her hand. It was alder wood, a wet wood that grew along the river and could not be used on the fire. Kablea's brother was the crafter of wood. To make the bowl he had repeatedly used embers from the fire to burn the inside of the stump. After each burning, he ground the inside with a flint chisel until it was smooth.

Zuri then went into the hut to collect deer bones that were resting on the hot stones of the fire. She could only handle them by holding the joint at the cooler end out of the embers. She placed them over a stone and shattered the ends with a mace head. The length of the bone had to be undamaged so that it could be used for making into tools. It needed just the right amount of force to make the bone crack near the joint; warm marrow started to trickle out. She caught this in a bowl and using a sliver, scraped out the inside, easing out the remainder.

The deer had fed them well over the past few suns. Both the matriarch and patriarch had ailing teeth so the soft organs were kept aside for them. Zuri took note of this now, aware that her baby would be weaned off the breast by eating the same food, the food of the old. Zuri had prepared the lungs, slowly beating them with a wood hammer to release all the breath, and using a small flint, she cut out the hard cartilage. The lungs, stomach, kidneys and liver, were all cooked in the pot until they were soft enough to be eaten by those who could not chew. The matriarch had boiled the blood and added barley grains to thicken the fluid. Food was plentiful at this time, the time of the rising sun.

It would not be long before the speckled fish would run the river. They were never certain when this would happen but it was at least two moons away. The red flesh of the fish and fish eggs were eagerly awaited. Their numbers were so great that they could be speared in the shallows. The shaman told stories of how the Great Bear would catch these fish, pawing them out of the water. Bears were not seen in the valley any more. Traders told of bears that still lived in the wildwood and their pelts and claws were sometimes bartered. Zuri's eyes were taken to the water meadow and the figures of men using an ard to turn the black soil, one pulling and one guiding. They had formed ridges and these were defined by the white seabirds making raucous cries as they squabbled over worms. She knew that by sunfall the men would be weary. She had worked on the ard and it had left her aching and sore. The traders spoke of lands where the farmers used cattle to draw the ard but nobody had tried that in the valley.

The river was a good place to be. That thought took her back to the wildwood, up from the river on the white hills, where there were no farmers. Her family were hunters but the animals were becoming scarce and with few kills, they did not eat well. This was why their women were so good at foraging food, finding it where other people could not. The wild animals suffered where people grew in numbers. She had been told that out on the white island, which she could see, all the big animals had been hunted and could no longer be found. The hunting families had all gone except for the few that sought only in the sea. The farmers were growing in number and that was because they knew how to store grain and so had food in the cold times. This meant that the farmers had the most children. They needed women and would send men to hunter families to exchange grain or meat for them. These women could only be exchanged before they had the flow of blood. When that time came, the farmers would put them through the ceremony to prepare them for the bearing of children. She knew that only women moved in this way and the male hunters could not make union with the women of the farmers. At first she was overwhelmed by this new life but other women on the river had been exchanged and told her how to fit in, how to be valued. Zuri found that the answer lay in her foraging skills. Although that sounded easy, it had shocked her that on the river many of the plants of the white hills did not grow. Worse, plants unknown to her were everywhere. She recalled her mother's mantra, that a plant once seen was always known and then readily found. Plants lived like people, in special places, where the Gods placed them. She saw the soil first; was it white or black, wet or dry? The different trees, their shape against the sky and their leaves and bark also told her about the soil. Every plant had its own hue and the plants formed groups of colour. She could sense where each of the food plants could be found. She also had skills that the farmers lacked. They did not set snares, even though these caught a leg or neck and did not puncture the skin of the animal with arrow holes. Traders preferred snared skins, and deerskin cloaks could only be made if the animal was snared, or caught in a pit trap. But pit traps had a nasty habit of catching people, so they could only be set in special places and had to be marked so that people knew where they were.

She also realized that she could handle pigs, because her family had regularly hunted and snared wild pigs. As the pig skins were eaten, not scraped for use as clothing, the hunters could shoot them with arrows. Even when the pigs were snared, the hunters still killed them by firing arrows at close range and told children to practice their bow skills on the snared pig. The pigs would then squeal even louder as the arrows pierced them. The farmers kept pigs but they were always wild and unmanageable. They would stay close to humans because they ate their poop, the fresher the better. They would hassle the children by running towards them when they squatted down in the fields to relieve themselves, and then immediately eat up their poop. A big stick was necessary to fend them off. It was also difficult to keep them out of the forest when acorns were in season. At least that kept them from grubbing up the fields, which the tribe had worked hard to clear of trees for the cattle to graze. Zuri sometimes managed the pigs, leaving the children to tend the cattle, which were less skittish. At night, all the stock had to be put into the pen which was surrounded by thorny branches to stop them wondering onto the ard ploughed areas. The dogs slept at the entrances to the huts to warn of any foxes or wolves that came near.

Her real challenge had been the sea. It was the first time she had seen it and the way it stretched beyond sight had frightened her. She knew the river from the few occasions that she had foraged down from the wildwood but had never needed to go into the water. Where she was born, a spring created a small stream and so she could not swim. She soon learnt and now water held no fear and offered so much food. She had never seen or eaten the fish and shellfish that she now ate often. Was it all this seafood that made their children so hale and strong?

Zuri now felt at one with the farming Gods down on the river. She had settled in well but other women told different stories. All the conflict and fights had happened over women or the lack of them. The patriarch had to mediate but all too often his words were not accepted and bitterness arose. At these thoughts she stopped scraping, her arm exhausted, and took the skin inside the hut to hang it up. She needed fibre so walked down to the river, lifted some stones and pulled skeins of lime tree bark out of the water. She tested its flexibility but found that it was still too stiff. She turned it over and pushed it back into the water, weighing it down again with the stones to keep it under the surface. The fibres were needed for making cord and lime bark was easily the best but it involved much labour. Back at the hut she pulled a large lime branch out of the woodpile. Using a flint chisel, she cut a single line into the bark and down the stem of the branch. It was a test of her nimble fingers, to slip a flint under the bark edge, tease it open and peel the bark off in long strips. It was these strips that she had to soak for some suns in order to release the long fibres. It was a task she had to repeat sun after sun until all the lime bark had been stripped and the remaining wood could then be used or burnt. She knew the lime by its leaves and yet she had never seen a fully grown tree since she had come down the valley. Here, they cut the branches down when they were the thickness of a man's arm. This happened when the sap flowed and the fresh leaves could be eaten by the cattle before the bark was stripped. There was no waste; the Gods forbad waste.

The light was fading and they would eat as soon as Kablea and his brother returned from using the ard. Kablea was taller than most, and thin, so they called him after the strong cord that they made. His brother Ereilea, the sower, was so named because of his skill in broadcasting seed; a well scattered seed thrived and led to a good harvest. The patriarch returned with them, and together with Ereilea's union and children, they all sat on the beds eating bowls of deer stew. Afterwards, they were given the boiled peewit eggs, the first the children had ever seen. They fondled them, and Zuri pointed out the intricate markings on the shell and how these made them so hard to find amongst the pebbles. It was the novelty of the eggs and not just the eating that gave them the most joy. Zuri made them all laugh when she mimicked the birds call, pee-wit, pee-wit, pee-wit.

In the darkness, as they sat around the fire, the women retold what they had heard from other women in the valley. Then the patriarch told them stories, of how the tribe had once moved with the deer and aurochs into the unending forests. How they could stay in one place for all time once they knew how to farm the land and rear animals. She felt secure as his words took her mind to the river and the sea, as if the land floated upon water. The patriarch had told them that the Gods were above, in the eerie silence, and had given them fertility and abundance. Zuri looked into the fire, sated and warm, as the smoke caused her eyes to seep water.

Chapter 8

The Fall of the Pagans

Zuri was a pagan, a word that has so many connotations. Its definition is vague and mostly used in a derogatory sense by adherents of the major religions to describe people with minority beliefs or with no beliefs. The pagan and the heathen were interchangeable words, and they threatened civilisation. In truth, the pagans of prehistory tended to be nature orientated and to have more than one God, to be polytheistic.

It would be easy to imagine that the battle between pagan beliefs and Christianity has been consigned to the past but that is not so. In recent decades, support for the Church of England has continued to decline and its doctrines and finances grow weaker by the year. The modern pagan, though they might not appreciate the use of the word, are those who are secular. In Britain these people are the majority and yet only a few step over the line and actually call themselves atheists. There is nothing in the definition of pagan to suggest that such people are unlearned, uncivilized or in any way lacking in their moral values simply because they do not possess the Ten Commandments.

This continuing battle, the contradictions as it were, between the Christian and pagan came to the fore when I attended the hustings in Christchurch for the last general election. Heavens, Zuri, you would have loved it, the biggest meeting of the gerontocracy for years (I am sorry, "heavens" is not a word that you would understand). It was in April 2015 and was organized by four local Christian churches. I thought of you, a pagan, and then I felt anxious for myself, an atheist. I realize that you don't know about Christianity but it's very similar to the spirit of the bear. Both beliefs require you to be afeared, a lovely old English word, of the righteous hand or clawing paw.

There were between 400 and 500 grey hairs in attendance and knowing that the gerontocracy dominates Christchurch, we can assume a high level of religiosity. Our Conservative MP, aware that this was the case, immediately flattered the audience by declaring that this was the only constituency in the UK with the word Christ in its name. He visibly glowed as he said this, as if Christianity was a significant yet unmentioned political influence in the party's manifesto; which it is. A number of questions were put to the panel of politicians. One related to how Christians feel under attack, not least because of national dictates barring the wearing of jewellery in the form of a cross, at their work. Yes Zuri, I know you sometimes wear a boar's tooth around your neck. Then a question was asked that suggested that Christians were disadvantaged more than gays; it was turning ugly. Fortunately, a political question pulled the audience away from something tantamount to bigotry. Bigotry, yes Zuri, that's the way the farmers demean the hunter-gatherers, and no, I am not going to explain gay.

I sat there, mulling over the historical perspective: is Christchurch a Christian centre? The number of people who call themselves Christian has halved since the 1960s and less than 1% of people now go to church on Sundays. Was I the only person in the room aware that we had at least 9000 years of pagan belief before the first church was built here in AD 800? Christianity has dominated for little over 1000 years and is relatively meaningless in the UK today, except in the Tory party and the Lords.

There was no chaos prior to Christianity; pagan society was successful and Zuri was part of that flourishing. Perhaps we should ask how much responsibility Christianity had for the destruction and denigration of our pagan past. Historians have often posited the theory that most early churches were placed over previous pagan sites. This was not new and replicated Roman strategy in lands that they occupied, including Britain. They knew that highly superstitious people would continue using ancient ritual sites so they integrated Roman pagan Gods with those venerated by the conquered, and gave the sites dual purpose. This way, they managed the sites, kept the local people in view and avoided underground movements developing. The late archaeologist Mick Aston of the Channel 4 Time Team and famous for his long hair and woolly Fair Isle jumpers, wrote that the early Christian missionaries under Mellitus in AD 602 were exhorted by Pope Gregory to utilize earlier pagan sites where new churches were being built. This ensured that people continued frequenting those places they had always used. Neither would it appear that the Christian faith was ruthlessly trying to obliterate old beliefs. Whatever, a church in wood was built in Christchurch in AD 800.

In Britain, pagan sites were feared by Christians as places of the black arts, particularly banks and ditches in the round, the more so if they included standing stones. We call these henges and they come in many forms but at its simplest, the people identified a circle or oval, cut a ditch around it and used the excavated soil to build a mound around the outside. The mound on the outside is not a defensive feature. It is the opposite of what is found at Iron Age hillforts, like Maiden Castle or Dudsbury Rings, where crossing the outside ditch exposes attackers to armed defenders atop the mound, or rampart, on the inside. Such hillforts were built thousands of years after the henges, as intertribal strife developed. Also, unlike with hillforts, as many as four entrances could be built across the henge ditch and into the inner circle. None of these entrances are defended by ramparts. A circle of stones was sometimes placed around the inside of the henge, often hundreds of years later. Few henges have been entirely excavated but it is evident that most included features inside that are no longer visible. These might have been small ritual buildings or wood circles created using huge tree trunks. The mound and the ditch may have acted as a threshold, a line across which one passed between two different worlds. The ditch may have been symbolic of water, a divide, and in wet weather might have routinely flooded. The mound may have connected with the heavens and the ditch with the underworld. The ditch at Avebury, for instance, was nine metres deep, steep sided and just reached the water table. What is certain is that the area inside the henge was a sacred space and had great significance. Most henge sites appear to have had a very long period of use, in various forms, little of which is fully understood. The henge is usually circular so does it reflect the sun or moon or represent a baby sac, a womb, the rotundity of pregnancy or even of fatness, itself a sign of robust health in otherwise thin people?

The henge also represented collective achievement, which would have appeared impressive, as if the physical labour involved in the construction had a spiritual dimension. The effort was individual, yet with a collective understanding that by working together the tribe could create great things. It can seem futile now, all that waste of energy to venerate what we might see as ineffectual Gods. Yet I can waste much effort exercising, driven by the God of fitness even though I am aware that it is endorphins, not supernatural spirits that feed my soul. Are we really very different, our people and Zuri's?

The fear of the standing stones in the last millennia has been very real and they were often completely removed from the landscape. At Avebury, a few hundred years ago, a number of the stones were buried up to three metres deep, well below what was necessary to simply obscure their presence. This was an example of overkill, a desire to put the stones so deep that they could not exert any supernatural power. At Avebury and many other circles, fires were built around the stones and when heated sufficiently, cold water was thrown over them and the shattered pieces then used for building and walling. The fact that henges and stone circles remain in the landscape at all suggests that the fear was sufficient for the more conservative and superstitious farmers to ignore them.

It was from an historian in Cumbria in the 1980s that I first heard of the theory that churches often overlay pagan sites. He had studied all the churches in the area and gave examples of circular churchyards evidently placed over a previous henge site. Proven examples of churches placed on pagan sites in Dorset are few with the most obvious at Charlton, north of Wimborne Minster, where the church sits inside a henge. St Catherine's church on the hill above Abbotsbury is an example of the difficulty faced extending this list. It sits on a flat platform and some experts have suggested this might have been a Neolithic henge or other sacred site. Similarly, Sopley church is situated on what might be seen as an artificial mound, which is also circular. This site is also a promontory created by the Avon and a small stream.

Clearly, Christchurch needed its own henge, but where was it? If we walk today across Quomps, now a park, the Priory can be seen from the west as crowning a distinct mound. Within the churchyard the circular outline of a henge is also easy to imagine. When the church was first proposed this would have been the ideal site. Initially, perhaps a small church sat in the middle of the henge as at Charlton. The deeply Christian Normans might well have expanded the Priory to wipe out all of the pagan features. Any standing stones will have been destroyed at an early stage.

The peninsula upon which the Priory sits has all the characteristics that such a henge would demand. It requires a surround of water and enough elevation so that it has an open view in all directions. People needed to see the rise and fall of the sun and moon and feel the four winds on their face. Any trees obscuring the view will have been removed.

Zuri's people will have animated this distinctive and very unusual location. She calls the spot Hartz Ahoa or the Bear's Head. She will hear all this from the shaman, the storyteller who specializes in the local myth of how a dead bear created this landform.

What adds weight to this henge theory is that no later Bronze Age burials appear to have been placed in or around the Priory site, which suggests that it was a pre-existing sacred location. The nearest identified burial location is further north on the peninsula. This is Latch Farm, which was close to or under the present Latch Farm Avenue, and was the site of a bell barrow. This was excavated prior to gravel extraction and the finds are featured in the Red House Museum. The barrow was circular, 33 metres across and had a surrounding ditch. The sand from the ditch was used to build the central mound. There were a few burials in the mound but the majority were placed in the ditch. In all, there were 90 urn burials of cremated remains, which is exceptional. These date to the Early Bronze Age, perhaps 200 years after Zuri's time. What the burials at Latch Farm show is that the area remained a centre of population in the Bronze Age. These burials represented the elite of that society because they were cremated and the ashes placed in urns. It is highly likely that this prominent domed barrow was visible from the River Avon, another status factor. It is also worth noting that Hengistbury Head, Wick, St Catherine's Hill and my street in Friars Cliff all have their ancient tombs whilst the peninsula, otherwise ideal for burial, was unused.

The area now under the Priory was a ritual zone of henges, perhaps wood circles or even much earlier constructions. We know that as towns like Christchurch developed, housing was erected on all the dry ground but rarely on pagan ritual sites, which were feared. Consequently, such places often remained as the only open space upon which the new church could be built. This needed an extensive area because the new church had to include a capacious churchyard, a sacred space into which the Christian dead could be embowered. Only Christianity had the confidence and the power to override the pagan influence, not least through the ceremony of consecration, first introduced around AD 900. The Bishop, God's representative, would walk around the perimeter of the site, strike his staff on the ground and place the land under the jurisdiction of the Holy See. The church, which later became the Priory can be seen for what it is, a continuation of the ritual use of the site, just another supernatural deity.

Archaeological displays in the Red House Museum suggest that a henge did exist on Hengistbury Head and was lost to sea erosion. The Head was across more extensive marshes then and, as now, was not readily accessible to people on the peninsula where Christchurch stands, or along the Avon.

For a clearer picture of how Avonlands centres on Christchurch, I imagined myself rising in a hot air balloon above the town. The Stour eases left and the silver ribbon of the Avon takes the eye northwards past Ringwood, beyond the recently located Temple complex at Damerham and on to Marsh Farm, near Breamore House. This is where the beautiful green jadeite axe was found, which had taken over 1000 hours to produce in the Italian Alps around 3000 BC, an axe head that would shatter with one blow if actually used. Further north I see Salisbury, where the river divides, the River Avon continuing north in the centre, the Wylye River turning west and the Bourne River heading east. The Avon passes through Durrington Walls to Upavon and then east adjacent to the massive henge at Marden, perhaps the most enigmatic and least understood henge the archaeologists have identified. As I gain height the land rises to the north but also rises left over Cranborne Chase to meet the River Stour, with another high area moving right to the Iron Age hillforts near Stockbridge. The entire area loosely forms a heart, its bottom tip sitting right on Christchurch; at the heart of the heart lies Stonehenge, with its avenue leading down to the river. That is no coincidence; the ritual heights link directly to the mythical river, the river of life, which links Stonehenge to the sea.

Avonlands is bisected, its pagan foot beneath Christchurch

Priory and towards its centre, Salisbury Cathedral. That is a lot of church for a small and insignificant area of heath and chalk. Initially, I was troubled that Salisbury Cathedral does not sit on an ancient pagan site. That was my mistake. Salisbury Cathedral, the first one, was a short distance north, sitting over the pagan summit of Old Sarum, an Iron Age hillfort even closer to Stonehenge. Old Sarum was the centre of population and pagan ceremony for that part of Avonlands, the reason why all the Roman roads later intersected with it. What we now know as Salisbury was damp and lush water meadows. It was over 200 years later that the church abandoned Old Sarum and moved down to the present cathedral site, where Salisbury township developed around it. The two great Christian houses in Avonlands were, after all, used to erase pagan sites. The irony is that it was actually the pagans who built the first "cathedral", called Stonehenge, and created the first common culture, the unified area of Avonlands.

As the pagan fell and the Christian rose, other forces conspired to break up Avonlands. Christchurch was part of Hampshire until 1974 when local government reorganisation relocated it in Dorset. That made sense as geographically it does not fit Hampshire and for centuries the route east was shut off by the Royal New Forest. Yet neither does Christchurch relate westwards to Bournemouth, that Victorian usurper having no history beyond a pier and bathing machines. Christchurch was always the guardian and servant of the Avon and Stour rivers, often severely compromised by the flooding of these errant forces. Geophysically, Avonlands was and remains naturally evolved to embrace every rivulet, spring and stream that flowed into the two rivers.

The pagans came from the sea and Christchurch was perhaps the first beach they landed on. They progressively moved up the rivers to the watershed, where they stopped, looking out over what we know as the Cotswolds to the north and Somerset and Devon to the west. Turning back, they saw the Avon running south towards the sun. They venerated the way the sun dominates Avonlands, coming up over its eastern perimeter and setting on its western. Moving down the river and its tributaries they looked south, they looked to the sun, and were bathed in light and warmth. Is it any surprise that the icon for Stonehenge was the sun? The tribe knew that they controlled the entire water catchment and that included all movement because it was based upon water. It cannot be overemphasized how this control reduced intertribal strife and made Avonlands a relatively peaceful place to live.

In considering prehistory, I had to ask myself what part pagan women might have played in their society. This was, of course, before the daughters of Eve had to be punished after the fall. What is evident is that during Zuri's time, women had highly ceremonial burials and in no way inferior to those of men. An elaborate Neolithic grave found on Cranborne Chase contained the body of a woman and three children, one of which was her own. Analysis proved that she was from the limestone Mendip hills, 80 kilometres north, yet the children were all raised on chalk soils and were probably local. All of them had iron deficiency anaemia even though the cause of death is unknown. Also, the cremated remains of a woman from the Late Bronze Age were found on Hengistbury Head under an elaborate burial mound. Such burials are unlikely if women had been treated as inferior or as chattels or even unclean, as they would be under Christianity. I even have to accept that my assumed Bronze Age warrior in my street might actually be a woman. The irony, if we accept that Zuri was emancipated in the Neolithic, is that in present day Britain some women, the Nirvana seekers, pursue spiritual faiths such as Buddhism. This is despite the fact that in countries where these faiths dominate, women are treated as second class citizens, as chattels.

Pagans, as with Christians, needed an intermediary between

them and the deities, somebody to manage ceremony. I decided that for Zuri this role should be a shaman and shamaness. I dismissed the use of a seer because it is a more restricted role, that of a prophet who sees into the future. Neither is soothsayer, augur or sibyl any more fitting. The shaman's spirit can leave his body to fly to other worlds and then return. He also controls fire. Many societies still have shamans and their storytelling reinforces the myths and helps people to understand their place in the world. Although existing shamans are male, there is no evidence to deny females undertaking this or a similar role. Zuri's shamaness is the expert in plant based potions and everything to do with illness and childbirth.

Pagans and Christians have been equally dependent upon rituals. Ritual is a construct that societies build up, a series of votive offerings asking for favour and benevolence from the Gods, perhaps for the rain to fall and the crops to grow. Because our seasons are so evident, summer and winter solstice have always been significant dates. As for Zuri's tribe, we can assume a ritual for each life event from birth to death, including the coming of age, manhood and womanhood. Her people left little evidence of warrior rituals. Had they done so, it might have been similar to the Masai in East Africa. Until recent times, they initiated young men into manhood by sending them out to kill a lion armed only with a spear. The spear and other weapons take precedence in such societies and yet my overview of English museums suggested an agrarian and rather passive society in Britannia. This contrasts with what I found in my planned visits to the national museums in Copenhagen and Stockholm. A quick visual scan of the linear development of Scandinavians after their Ice Age, which was more recent than ours because they are more northerly, was telling. Cabinets full of weapons immediately intimidate, most especially the daggers, in flint and stone and then bronze. The warrior culture ruled in these areas and the Viking male, aggressive and invasive of our peaceful farming cultures, evolved. We can assume that in our more passive society, women were treated as equals. It was not a conscious decision rather than just the natural order.

Zuri's tribe have an image of the cosmos and how it is structured. The sun and the moon represent the upper sphere, the land of the living the middle sphere and the underworld, the zone of the dead, lies beneath. The henge circle is their immunity and their rituals summon up spirits from within the ditch, the gap into the underworld. If I imagine Zuri within her henge of Hartz Ahoa some 4000 years later, she would find herself inside the Priory. Would she be able to follow a service? The sun and moon are replaced by heaven, the abode of one God. The Holy Spirit is called into presence and asked to watch over the dead, whose underworld is now called paradise. The black spirits are now the devil, who is vilified and the congregation is told to avoid the tools of his trade; fornication. Okay, I accept that Zuri might not understand that one. There are also places in the Priory reserved for the exclusive use of the clergy just as there are places in the henge where only the shaman or shamaness can perform ceremony.

The sophistication of these belief patterns tell us that it is disingenuous to infer that the pagans are lesser beings and uncivilized. With no concept of sin, Zuri can watch the young women celebrate coming of age within the henge, and see sexuality as life affirming and childbirth as the means by which the tribe measures its success. She knew how the henges and Stonehenge had evolved and what they meant to her society; how the tribe's forebears had dug ditches and hauled and worked stones. That this was a form of reciprocity; you labour for the Gods to gain their favour and it led to the foundation of a successful tribe.

Perhaps the question remains: Can Christchurch reclaim its pagan heritage? As a Christian and conservative town, it is doubtful. It is only when the pagan and Christian heritage is given equal weight that we are free to venerate prehistory as worthy. Yet, here we are, with all our knowledge, no better than Zuri as we use stories, which we call science fiction, to construct our universe.

Chapter 9

Celestial Sisters

Zuri read the signs and the burgeoning tide told her the moon was full. As for the sun, the sky cleared and she knew that the two sisters were to meet. As the sun fell, the slow drumbeat summoned everyone down to Hartz Ahoa. The warm wind was from the south and on it floated the ever louder beat, mingled with the aroma of the sea. At the circle, they sat on the bank and silently waited. Looking out across Hartz Ahoa and the high water, the smoke curled lazily up from huts on the Hill of the Bear's Arm, before it was snared by the breeze sweeping over the cliffs beyond. Turning to the west, beyond the marshes, the low sun prepared to drop into the underworld.

Since moving to the valley she had taken part in the ceremony that was about to occur. Back in the wildwood she had heard the story of the two sisters but it had made no sense. The Gods of the wildwood had protected hunters and the animals and it had never occurred to her that farmers had different Gods. Some Gods gave them good harvests whilst others protected women and animals when giving birth. Farmer's desired fertility and that the baby sac was ever full; that more life was a favour the Gods could bestow and when it happened the tribe could only grow stronger. Zuri felt part of this fertile world and protected by the two sisters.

She looked into Hartz Ahoa, her eyes alighting on the great cove in the centre, which she had helped to rebuild not five moons ago. The old cove had rotted away and everyone who was strong enough had played a part. What had surprised her was that the less strong, the older people, had joined them, keen to do some work, no matter how small because any effort on Hartz Ahoa would be known to the Gods. The ancestors would also know this and their place in the underworld would be secure. The farmers paid homage to their Gods through the construction of a henge, unlike her people in the wildwood, who worshipped their Gods through the animals. Yet the cove had demanded much in its rebuilding. Five tall straight trees had been selected upriver and then anointed by the shaman. The bark around each standing tree had been hacked off with axes so that they died upright, became leafless and were left to bleach white in the sun. They were then felled, stripped of their branches and floated down the river before being dragged up to Hartz Ahoa. She, and others, had laid down slimy seaweed upon which to haul the heavy trunks up the slope.

Whilst the timbers were being brought down the river she had worked on the five round postholes that were needed, each side by side but in a curve to form a half circle. The holes were narrow and deep, and sometimes they had to work lying down, head first, into the hole. Small children had to drop into the bottom to remove the spoil. They had used antler picks to dig and when they had finished one of the picks was broken and placed at the bottom of one of the holes. Zuri had gone head first into that hole, so determined was she to touch the antler before it went under the timber. The broken tool was a token of their regret, their apology for having cut into the underworld, for their intrusion. Was it her work on the cove or that touching that she now carried a child?

The digging of each posthole had been overseen by the shaman. He marked the circular hole first, and then made depressions to show where the slot should be cut into the side. The timber would be guided down into the hole by the slot. He was insistent that each timber had to be placed into its own hole. It was a union and the Gods would know if it was wrong. There was a celebration when the timber was finally dragged to the slot and hauled upright using ropes. As it went skywards, the timber slid down the slot and dropped into the hole. It was like the fit of the shaft into a stone mace, which had to be neat and tight. The shaman then shouted instructions to the people on the ropes, as his eyes told him how to position each timber in the sky, upright and the same distance apart. Only then would the soil be carefully placed and rammed hard but always in the same order in which it had been removed. The spirits of the underworld were watching.

The five timber posts rooted in the underworld linked with the two spheres; the land and the sky were in union. The shaman said the Gods might give a sign to show that this work was good. During great storms, streaks of white fire from the sky had hit the posts and passed down into the underworld. When that happened, the wood had turned black and scorched and people came from all over to see the power of the Gods.

Zuri stopped musing as the shaman appeared, his small body bulked across the shoulders by a cape of beaver pelts. He moved like an animal because he was an animal, a beaver that went under water, lived in and knew the underworld. He glided along the bottom of the ditch, chanting into the cleft and imploring the spirits to join them. He held an axe in his left hand and an auroch's bone in the other. The skin of his eye sockets were blackened with charcoal so that his eyes peered out, shining more like those of an eagle than a man, penetrating and shrewd.

The drumbeat changed as the shamaness stepped forward for the ceremony of the two sisters. She led the maidens across the causeway on the sunrise side. They faced the falling sun as they entered the circle. Each maiden wore a single seashell, the home of the shellfish with so much fertility that it became uncountable in number. Zuri had been one of these maidens not many moons ago until she had gone through this initiation as an unbearer. Now, with her first baby inside her, she would become a bearer in a few moons.

The shamaness looked to the sun, raised her arms and summoned its glowing orb down into Hartz Ahoa. She called upon the sun to hear her words, that between its waking and sleeping to shine upon the maidens and give them strong bodies and many children. The failing light put a pink glow on the wood at the back of the cove, which showed its open arc only to the rising sun. The shamaness walked the maidens around the outside of the circle and out by the causeway on the sunset side. There, they waited to meet the sun's sister.

As the sun fell the cove cast its shadow. Seabirds perched on the top of the posts, mewed, and looked down at the people. The birds carried spirits and were part of the ceremony until the crackling fire was lit in the centre of the circle. The birds flew away and everyone became still and silent. The blood red sky faded and they looked east to a faint glow over the white island. The full moon crept up over the darkling hills to display its glowing face; it was the sister of the sun. Zuri was in awe of the moon, the cold orb, with its strange light. Under its glow, she could feel its spirit and see the eerie shadow it cast over the land. Here, the farmers always knew the moon by the swell of the sea and only planted seed when it was at its fullest, when the sea swept hard up the river.

The shamaness brought the maidens around to the sunrise causeway and back into the circle in front of the cove. The cove of the morning sun was also the cove of the moon, as it laid its chill glow into the recess formed by the timbers. Each maiden in turn, walked into the cove, where the moon picked out her face. A glob of blood was placed on each forehead by the shamaness. She called upon the two sisters to unite and give them fertility, and then led them out across the sunset causeway. Zuri knew that they must not leave by the path they entered, because they were now unbearers and their families could now find a union for them.

Later, Zuri entered the warm hut filled with people sitting around the walls. So many people made the smoke worse and she coughed, as did others. When the shaman put green pine branches on the fire, the resinous smoke stung their eyes. Whenever, wherever, pine was put on a fire, she could see the shaman even when he was not there. This filled her with fear. If she could see him then he could see her, he knew where she was, what she was doing, what she was thinking. The shaman had visions of animals, birds and great creatures, some that people had never seen. Before he spoke, he lit the seal fat in his chalk bowl. The flame flickered around the hut as he placed his jadeite axe, with some ceremony, on the ground in front of him. The axe astounded all who saw it. It was polished so smooth and was the colour of the sea. It had great power because the stone was wrought from towering mountains far away, so high that they were always covered in snow and ice. Because it was made for the Gods it could never be used as an axe. Nobody else was allowed to touch it and so they never felt its substance. People said that it controlled the shaman's mouth and he could tell stories only after he had placed it upon the ground. The instant he stopped talking, he would pick it up, wrap it in a skin and put it away.

He then swallowed a potion, arched his back and contorted as he breathed out hard and harsh. This was the spirit coming out of his breath. His body baulked up, his arms became wings and he spoke of flying with the hookbeak birds beyond the bright sun and the cold moon.

Zuri knew she would remember all this and recount the stories to her children. She could imagine them around her, listening intently, learning about the animals and their world. She would tell them about the Great Bear, how he had reigned over the freezing lands and had begged the Gods for the warmth of the sun. After a great battle the Gods had relented on the condition that he sacrificed himself, that he fall from the place of the Gods and down to earth. This he did and his body was turned into the warm and fertile land, his head became Hartz Ahoa and his outstretched arm the hill. His legs gouged out the land where the Gods released the springs of sweet water from the underworld to form the rivers and keep them flowing. His eyes had shot out and fallen over the edge of the world. One eye returned as the warming sun and the other as its sister, the moon, to give them the tides and fertility. Zuri fell asleep that night with thoughts of how the baby within her would one day listen to these stories.

Chapter 10

Bearing in Bear Country

Children in Friars Cliff are relatively rare creatures. Neither was the subject of birth on my agenda when I began writing this book. The gerontocracy and birth are not bedfellows, the menopause has switched us off and consequently, there is no midwifery unit in Christchurch. Mortality is far more significant to the town, not least those in the business community who provide coach-built vehicles, imported flowers, a sombre haute couture and ceremonies. I'm talking funerals, of course.

Yet, as I have become more enlightened through my research, I have come to appreciate that Zuri must have children; it is her main purpose in life, her agency for the Gods. A woman who did not give birth was blighted, seen to have offended the deities and would have lacked status.

As you will have noted, I have not defined marriage as such. Zuri was brought or is it bought in by the farmers because worldwide this seems to have been a pattern in early societies. I could have described her as a migrant providing sex, another universal theme, but these issues are outside my remit. Certainly, there was no moral need for a marriage contract or for a marriage ceremony. The child, however or by whomever it was conceived, would have had equal value under their benevolent Gods and I don't believe any child would have been labelled a bastard. However, the family and the elders will have set out rules, called mores, and controlled the sexual liaisons by sheer force of will. The young will have acceded to these mores because anyone trying to deny them might, if not cast out, find themselves ostracized.

The gerontocracy is no different from Zuri's elders in their desire to have grandchildren. Our aged angst comes to light through an increasing number of daughters and sons, some with gay and lesbian predilections, who are unable or unwilling to provide a grandchild. I can understand this because here I am, childless, perhaps feeling a touch virtuous, aware that the present world is dying from over population. The irony is that I am now an advocate for Zuri, who 4000 years earlier is unfulfilled, perhaps even damned, if she does not produce a child.

The bank of mum and dad is now a gerontocracy cliché and you might expect me to excoriate rich grandparents who spoil the young. That would be a mistake. Zuri might be on her own as regards the National Health Service and modern science but she too is sheltered within an extended family. Her elders need and want her to succeed but perhaps the difference is that they have a narrower vision of success. That is a steady supply of babies, who are healthy, who can grow up to work and have more babies. Added to environmental good fortune, which is decent weather and good harvests, the future is bright for the family group. What amazes me is the similarity between the gerontocracy and Zuri's elders, how little has changed over 4000 years. It might even be considered that the challenges today make the situation far worse for the gerontocracy. It wants grandchildren to be protected against adversity and has the resources to achieve this. Yet success, measured by university degrees and annual earnings, creates opportunities that discourage childbearing. An interesting career, money, perhaps power, can make the humdrum of childrearing unappealing and it is no surprise that birth rates in Europe have plummeted. Even those who want children cannot because the sperm count has fallen by one third between 1989 and 2005. Increasing numbers of people need medical intervention to achieve pregnancy and birth.

For Zuri to survive childbirth she would have needed a normal birth. In 2017 the Royal College of Midwives reported that about four in ten women give birth normally, down from six in ten in the 1980s. A normal birth is without caesarean section, induction of labour, instrumental delivery or epidural. The RCM further stated that a normal birth, also called a natural birth when no drugs are used, meant that some women were seeing the words as suggestive of failure if medical intervention becomes necessary. A normal birth is now to be called a physiological birth. The trigger for all this is the rising caesarean rate, up from 10% two decades ago, to 27% today. Zuri would not understand the medical control that modern women have experienced. This is especially true when there is unnecessary medical intervention that causes physical and psychological trauma to both mother and baby.

As for the gerontocracy, if motherhood or indeed fatherhood is no longer an aspiration for their children and grandchildren then other challenges lie ahead. The gerontocracy denigrates the kind of work Zuri will have done, the dirty hands of horticulture, labouring and even farming. There is now an expectation of a university degree and a profession. Some of these children will spend a lifetime in academia. Unlike Zuri, they have to experience cognitive dissonance, the challenge of so much opportunity and so many decisions. What do I want to do and what do my parents and grandparents expect me to do? Consequently, we see high levels of mental illness, dietary issues and increasing suicides. In Zuri's narrow world the expectation on the child was simply to replicate the parent.

Today, with a low birth rate and high aspirations, we need immigrants to do our dirty work. The irony is that it is the wealthy gerontocracy that employs them as gardeners and carers who also consider immigration to be a social ill. The correlation in Zuri being an outsider is interesting. She brought in different skills and if her hunter-gatherer family were different to the farmers, new DNA. Over 4000 years the conditions might have changed but not the principal.

The modern concept of love or romance would have been a luxury that Zuri would not have experienced. The sex organs would have been a utility subservient to the higher need of creating a baby, the means by which the tribe and their culture survives. That is not to say that an orgasm could not be enjoyed and it would have kept the men calm and orderly. As for becoming pregnant, Zuri knew of cycles and that her monthly blood and the lunar cycle closely matched at around 28 days, too coincidental not to be the agency of the Gods. The position of the moon would have told her when it was due and whether she was pregnant, or not. There is also the question of timing the pregnancy because having a baby in midwinter carries more risk. A birth in spring would allow mother and baby the relative ease of summer. There would be maximum food as well as a reduction in wasted energy producing body heat, this energy being diverted into the mother's milk. Was the spring festival, now May Day, typically a fertility rite, the time of union, of copulation? It is a date easily measured by the appearance of spring flowers. Assuming their fecundity as good, Zuri would note her absence of a period by June and know that the birth was due in nine moons, in what we call March.

I considered whether Zuri would formally practice sexual abstinence. That might also highlight her equality, the ability to make such a decision. Abstinence could also be a tribal more. An author researching farming in Herefordshire in the 1920s found that abstinence was commonly practiced between Advent and Candlemas (December to January). This was to ensure that women were not heavily pregnant at harvest time, when their labour was essential. Would Zuri have abstained from copulation from January to May to avoid giving birth between November and February? Unlike today, sex would not have been an indulgence to be taken lightly.

The death of a woman within the extended family would have been a tribal disaster so the shamaness and women experienced in birth will have devised a strategy to ease the birth process and reduce trauma. That said, deaths during childbirth are high in most undeveloped societies and I doubt it was any different in Zuri's time. Women almost certainly lived shorter lives than men and data shows this to have continued through the Victorian period and until after the Second World War. Yet Zuri still possessed some advantages over modern women that will have eased the birth process. Firstly, she was slim and fit with lithe muscles. Secondly, the baby will have been of a lower weight than is usual today. Thirdly, a considerable reduction in pelvic inlet depth has occurred in women since Palaeolithic times and this has made birth increasingly difficult. The cause is uncertain but it is suggested that the new diet of starchy grains brought about by farming contributed to this. Zuri's pelvic inlet depth was better than women today but smaller than women of the earlier Palaeolithic period.

In many undeveloped societies the woman must give birth alone, with no help, yet this never appeared a British trait. A hut reserved for birth was usual in many ancient societies as it enabled the other women in the tribe, those experienced in birth, to remove the labouring woman from stress and to keep her warm. They did not know that a baby in the womb cannot shiver and is highly susceptible to cold, but the need for warmth appears a given. Warmth, unfortunately, also meant smoke and poor air quality in the hut. It is also likely that Zuri will have been encouraged to frequently change her position in labour to alleviate pain and discomfort. Giving birth whilst lying flat, a practice introduced to suit the male obstetrician in modern times, both slows the process and inhibits the circulatory and pulmonary system. She would instinctively have used gravity to assist the birth, by kneeling or squatting.

They would have understood that breastfeeding was essential. Its greatest benefit is in its immediate availability and preventing the baby coming into contact with water-borne infections before being suitably weaned. To maintain lactation the baby must breast feed on demand, at least every four hours. This level of lactation also releases hormones that prevent ovulation and further pregnancy, providing the mother has not menstruated since her delivery. This process, of avoiding another pregnancy too soon after birth, is now called lactational amenorrhea.

How long Zuri breastfed is unanswerable. The current average in undeveloped countries is a surprising four years, especially if there is no access to clean water. Zuri also needed to work so would have kept the baby within her clothing and against her warm skin. Her baby could feed when it wanted and she would sense when it needed to urinate or defecate and hold the baby away from her at such times.

Did sexual contact continue after the birth? In some tribes, the men and women are parted to ensure the woman does not become pregnant for up to four years. Zuri's tribe probably recognized that too many babies weaken both mother and child, and rules on abstinence may have existed.

At least Zuri is a pre-Christian woman and so she has never fallen or known evil. As a pre-Eve, she is not to be punished by painful childbirth but it will be painful, nonetheless. Rituals will have dominated the entire process, with some specific to entering the birth hut, some for the lead up to and during the birth and to celebrate a successful birth. They would have ensured that she had adequate food and avoided food that might upset her, such as shellfish. To satisfy their superstitious nature they would have worn charms, amulets or ritual clothing.

Was the umbilical cord cut or left intact? The experts are split so I take the latter view. What happened to the placenta? Rituals around the world vary and there is no universal practice. Even today, there are some people who advocate the mother eating the placenta. Recent research proves that there are no nutritional advantages to this but in any society where starvation looms the placenta can be seen as valuable food. This assumes that the placenta is not given ritual significance whereby it would probably have been ceremoniously buried. When the woman returned to society and when the child was named, a ceremony could be anticipated. A dead baby would not be unusual and an established ritual would be ready when that happened, as well as when the mother herself died.

Zuri knew that birth could be difficult and there would be a number of plant preparations ready for the anticipated problems. The evidence for plant preparations date little earlier than the books called medieval herbals, which describe how to prepare potions. Goldenrod, once called woundwort, could have been applied to skin tears and other wounds. Raspberry is a native plant, which Zuri calls blood berry and the leaves are an ancient remedy for childbirth and menstrual problems. Cowslip flowers were used for headaches and other pain. Once gathered, these plants had to be slowly dried, out of the sun and stored in skin bags for later use. According to the season there were many other plant alternatives available in or around Christchurch and many of these will have been traded.

As to how Zuri gave birth I have to make some assumptions. The first is that the cord is not cut with a piece of flint, the technology of the day, and that the placenta is expelled naturally. When the baby first suckles this stimulates the uterus to contract, helps to expel the placenta and control bleeding. Today, this is called a lotus birth with the umbilical cord falling off naturally between three to ten days after the birth, the time dependent upon the humidity of the air. Zuri lived by the river and sea so it would be sooner rather than later. At birth, when the cord is left uncut, it pulsates for some minutes and valuable blood, high in iron, passes to the baby. These babies have less instances of bleeding in the brain and severe infections of the bowel. This was noticed as early as 1801 by Erasmus Darwin, the eminent doctor and grandfather of Charles Darwin. So for Zuri, the baby, cord and placenta will be kept together against her body: the gerontocracy is aghast.

What if the child was born with functional disabilities? In

ancient Greece we know that such babies were immediately put outside and left to die. That happened in all the Greek city states and not just in Sparta, which is a common belief. A deformed or disfigured baby was considered as rejected by the Gods. Death for them was not to be feared as it is by many of the gerontocracy. It would not have been any different in Avonlands, as no tribe could have maintained unproductive people. We might anticipate that mental retardation may have been low in Avonlands for three reasons. The first is that fish and seaweeds, which are full of iodine, are readily available. The second is that Zuri's bowl of cow's milk is also iodine rich, and the third, that food grown in soil near the sea contains iodine. Imbecility can be due to iodine deficiency and was common inland until recent times. Even today, up to 60% of people can be iodine deficient, particularly those opposed to dairy produce and this can impair mental and physical development. Pregnant women need almost twice as much iodine as people in general. This is another qualification for Avonlands appearing a paradise to these early people. Even their crops grew alongside the sea and tidal river, so were rich in iodine and had higher nutritional levels than when grown inland. The sea carrot abounds along our shore, its flower often covered in soldier beetles. We consider it no more than a humble wildflower, yet to a pregnant Zuri it was little less than manna in a pagan paradise. Their diet was also rich in omega 3 and this would have enhanced their intellect. Did these highly nutritious foods really create Stonehenge?

Compare Zuri to pregnant women today with their access to ample food but with dubious nutritional levels. The hybridization of crops, grown more for bulk than flavour, also means that we need to eat many times what Zuri ate in order to obtain the same level of minerals like iron. Our pregnant women are served by an industrialized food industry that relies on cheap corn syrup from the US, starchy modern flour, even palm oil and masses of salt purely to enhance flavour. Our babies enter a world in which the words local and natural are no longer relevant.

Chapter 11

To Us a Pagan Child is Born

Zuri felt heavy and uncomfortable. She walked with some difficulty past the hut where she would give birth, aware that she must not enter it, not without the shamaness being present. There was no opportunity anyway because the shamaness was inside, caring for Zooman. He had been felling trees and another man's flint axe had snapped off and hit him on the arm, tearing the flesh and much blood had flowed. The shamaness would apply a compress of woundwort. Zuri knew the plant and had collected the leaves in autumn, when the flowers, like tiny suns, shouted their presence. The leaves would be heated in a little water, applied to the wound and held in place by curved pieces of bark bound with nettle cord. It was awkward work for the fingers but it always staunched the blood and helped wounds heal. She knew that if her skin tore during the birth the same compress would be applied. Did the shamaness have enough of the dried leaves as it was not an easy plant to forage? Her thoughts about the plant and its healing power calmed her.

As she returned to the family hut she could hear the quernstone being pushed back and forth, a sound that now made her feel queasy. When her belly was large and she was told that she must stay around the hut, she tried to grind the grain each day. But, leaning forward over the quern, holding the handstone and grinding the grain had felt so uncomfortable. She had to look to herself and not put her belly under pressure but it troubled her not to do her usual work.

Two suns later she leaned over the fire and used a piece of wood to scoop up a small hot stone and drop it into her bowl of milk. It spread its heat, bubbling the white fluid. The milk had been reserved for her, its animal strength to build her up for the birth. As she leaned forward, awkwardly, she was aware of wetness between her legs. The women had told her to be watchful and here it was, the streaks of blood. It was the first sign that her baby was ready and belly pains would follow. She checked again, just to be certain and then told the matriarch, who sent word to the shamaness and to Mizda, the woman who would be with her during the birth. Zuri felt nervous and the matriarch, sensing this, talked about how the waiting would soon be over, that in a few suns the baby would come into their world. Her belly started to ache just as the next sun was rising and the ache soon became a pain. There were long periods between each pain up to the high sun but as the sun fell they became more intense and more frequent. The birth was getting closer.

It was now that the shamaness arrived and supported Zuri as they walked down to the birth hut. Outside its portal the shamaness passed a shell across Zuri's forehead and said "I call upon the twin sisters, the sun and the moon, to give this unbearer her first child, within this sheltered space, a child with lusty breath and voice, to join us in this world before it moves to the underworld. I call upon the twin sisters to drive out the dark spirits that might shelter inside and to keep the baby from harm." Zuri noted the words first child and fear grew within her because she knew that the first was the most difficult. They entered the hut with Mizda, a bearer of many children and so shown to have the blessing of the Gods. Her wisdom would keep bad spirits away from Zuri. She knew when to act and when to be quiet and still. Zuri felt protected, aware that nobody would enter the hut unless bidden by the shamaness.

The pains increased one upon another and built in intensity. To ease the pain she constantly moved. She walked, she sat, she rocked and she knelt. Mizda wiped the sweat from her naked body and gave her blood berry water to sip and to ease the pain. The gush of water, when it suddenly erupted from between her legs, was a shock. She watched it pool upon the floor. The pain quickly became more intense so she leaned on the wood bar, its posts anchored in the ground in the middle of the hut. Her fingers, white knuckled, gripped the bar and she realized its smoothness was due to the hands of the many women who had gone before her.

The pain grew in intensity and frequency and seemed not to ease. Her world of open skies and the sounds of life contracted into her frail and hurting body with a pain that seemed unending. The sweet taste of the blood berry water now tasted sour and she ejected it back into the bowl. Just when she thought that she could no longer endure the pain and discomfort, she felt an overwhelming need to expel the baby. It was as if it had decided that it no longer wanted to be part of her. With an involuntary urge to bear down, she grasped the bar even tighter, squatted and pushed. There was a relief in the effort because it bore an inner strength, that it was both an ending and a beginning. She was silent; nobody would hear her cry out. Her hand reached to feel between her legs where the skin was beginning to stretch and burn. She could touch the baby's head, yet it felt no bigger than a bird's egg. Then, there was more pain and an even greater urge to push. She could feel the head protruding further and knew that it must soon come to an end, yet the pain continued. Why was the head so slow to come? Fear welled up inside her; what if the baby was without breath? She had seen women emerge from the hut with a lifeless baby in their arms. She recalled a baby sent down into the underworld, nestled inside a white wing from a dead swan. There was despair when a woman lost her first child, the Gods had abandoned her and she would be anxious; only a live child could make her well again. She grasped her boar's tooth talisman, then looked at Mizda, who smiled as if she knew Zuri thoughts; all was well.

At the height of the next pain she pushed and the baby's head was out between her legs. She could not see the face, only the back of the head but with the next push the head turned to the side and she could see the glint of the eyes. They opened and closed in response to the soft light. The pain, the effort, everything froze in the blinking eyes of this new life. With the next expulsive force, the shoulders and body were squeezed out. With the expansion of the chest the baby gasped its first breath, which Mizda then said was the spirit entering the child. Cradling the baby, Mizda passed him into Zuri's arms. She sat back in utter joy and relief as she looked at the wet, blood smeared baby and understood that it too had suffered. She admired its wholeness and saw that it was a male child. She then lifted the baby to her nipple and he suckled lustily. As he did so, it triggered another pain inside her belly and the thick pulsating cord that hung between her legs, lengthened and with a gush of blood, the afterbirth slid out. Mizda was again ready and caught it, placing it inside a skin pouch, which she tucked up with the baby. The baby, the cord and the afterbirth remained as one. As the baby suckled, Zuri felt her belly tighten and Mizda said that this would lessen her bleeding. She looked at the baby, stunned by her new role as a bearer. She gazed at him, touched him, felt his warmth and his breathing and knew that everything, all that she had ever been, had led her to this moment. She suddenly felt exhausted and the effort of the birth flowed over her.

The shamaness was called to the hut, where the baby's strong suckle told her that all was well. She gave thanks to the twin sisters and called upon them to give the baby strength and agility and for Zuri to bear many more children.

Zuri slept deeply that night, with her new baby and the afterbirth nestled against her. The baby suckled at will and she was overwhelmed by his sweet milky odour and warmth. Kablea, her union, came to see the baby and marvelled at his health. Zuri watched his face as he spoke of how the baby would protect their future; the Gods were with them. Other women came to see the baby and told of their births but Zuri heard little and saw little other than her new child.

After two suns, Zuri had to present her baby to the ancestors at Hartz Ahoa. With the shamaness she walked around the circle, stopping where they had entered. Looking into the ditch of bare earth, into the underworld, Zuri lifted the baby out, to be seen, keeping the afterbirth close and without tension on the cord. The shamaness then called upon the ancestors to see the newborn and witness how the Gods had favoured it with life and strength.

Zuri was kept rested and fed by the matriarch so that her milk would become abundant. During this time she became aware of her new standing as a bearer; no longer a newcomer or outsider. After four suns, the birth cord and placenta separated from the baby and the pouch was hung in the roof of the hut, away from the dogs. Some suns later, the shamaness took the pouch and placed it in the midden because it possessed spirits that would pass down into the underworld.

After some suns Zuri returned to foraging, the baby in a sling clinging to her breast. Just like the cattle, he quickly found the nipple as and when he needed. When he wanted to empty himself, she sensed his movement, a tension in his body and eased him out to expel upon the ground. Every woman she met wanted to tell her how to be a bearer. That she must not eat food like wood garlic, which would taint her milk. When he cried loudly she was fearful. Keeping him well dominated each sun. He was now the focus of the family and they would watch over him. Every face smiled. In many moons the patriarch would give him a name and his name would come out of his body. It would reflect his ways, his features, his strength or speed, all that the Gods had given him. For Zuri, each sun was new and joyful.

Chapter 12

A Place of our Own

Farming began in Avonlands around 4000 BC and by Zuri's time her people had been building huts for perhaps 1800 years. She could not have envisaged how the utility of a hut could morph into the status implicit in a brick bungalow at the seaside. That retired people could spend well over £500,000 on a hut or that such equity could exist and be transferred to their children. It would seem unbelievable to her that the view of The Needles from the hut could increase the value by hundreds of thousands of pounds. It then occurred to me that the way the gerontocracy assist their children with home purchase is not dissimilar to the way Zuri was supported in the construction of a hut.

Yet, when we compare Avonlands today to Zuri's time, some profound changes are evident. The greatest change is in the status and impact of farming. In Zuri's time, Avonlands was at the cutting edge of farming. Some experts suggest that it was a lack of land in the Paris basin that forced skilled farming families to migrate to places like Avonlands. Whatever, life was good on the river, people flourished and spread.

Avonlands, perhaps the oldest farmland in the country, was later joined by the areas that could only be farmed after iron was invented. Together, these areas created Britannia, a farming powerhouse. Farming dominated from that time onwards, perhaps even driving the Roman and Norman invasions and reached its zenith after the Second World War. Farming in Britain, by then, was political and in all rural areas in the 1950s, the farming grandees would elect a Tory MP and write his bucolic script for Westminster. Yet, within my lifetime a revolution has occurred, which also changed Avonlands for the first time in perhaps 5000 years; the farming lobby lost all of its power. The industry today represents little more than 1% of GDP. It is not for me to blame the growth of cities or industry or even the rise of the socialists but the fact is that we now utilize supermarkets for our food and no longer have a meaningful relationship with the land. Farming is just another business left to the machinations of the market. Avonlands and its rural township called Christchurch went through this scenario. For the first time since Zuri's farming revolution, the employment and income power of cattle, sheep, chickens, orchards, wood and woods, beer and crops and the farmers market, has locally evaporated, eviscerated by global conglomerates.

As farming declined, Christchurch along with so many other rural towns lost its rural status. Progressively, it saw the closure of its cottage hospital, telephone exchange, mill, the wood yard next to the railway station, the police station and many of the functions of the town hall. All rural towns have diminished, no longer the heartbeat of their hinterland and little more than picture postcard places for townies to live, towns like Christchurch. The skills of the town, such as in timber, brewing, roofing, nursing, policing, these all existed in Zuri's time but not centrally. With no towns or villages the skills were practiced in huts scattered throughout Avonlands, they existed but on a much smaller scale.

Christchurch is now a troubled place, depleted after losing its farming hinterland and yet not a traditional seaside resort. It has been overwhelmed by Bournemouth, its upstart vulgar neighbour and reduced to a suburb, a retreat for those of the gerontocracy who revile an address in a mere seaside town with its saucy postcards. Yet the gerontocracy have created a new industry, that of home improvement, with its in vogue plastic cladding, roller garage doors, French oak floors, granite worktops and as the muscles in the legs weaken, Stannah stairlifts. With a moribund economy and diminishing returns from investments, financial advisors now suggest that improving your hut, perhaps adding extensions, offers the greatest return. They would certainly advise against investing in farming.

In the early 2000s there was a theory that single level living, Zuri's approach, was the way forward and yet true bungalows, perhaps an icon of Christchurch, are slowly disappearing. They are overwhelmed by the investment opportunity in the loft space. Bungalows morph into houses with four or more bedrooms and the value increases. The retired couple, the lifeblood of the town, find their horizons growing smaller as fewer and fewer two or three bedroom bungalows remain. The council, deprived of their farming generated income, reduce their horizons and sell beach huts. How parochial is that? The income presumably saves them from meltdown in a world-wide recession.

Thinking of the beach huts takes me back to Zuri. As parents' age and die it is natural to concede to the growing power of the next generation, those who have become bearers, successfully growing families. With this in mind, I felt that Zuri deserved a place of her own, what we have now demeaned as a hut. Yet, I ask myself what sort of hut they would build for her in prehistoric Christchurch. The housing situation circa 2200 BC has given me a few headaches. Firstly, no evidence of huts has been found in our locality and I am forced to utilize what has been found elsewhere, which is fairly sparse. In general, when an archaeologist exposes some post holes that suggest a round or rectangular building they seek evidence that it was a place in which people lived. A hearth, usually central, is a good start. Confirmation arises if a midden, the waste pit for ash, broken pottery and such is found adjacent to the hut. Strange as it might appear, the evidence shows that Zuri's people regularly swept the floor, not that we have recovered any besoms. They used flint tools for so much work that we can assume that many small pieces of flint readily broke off, each capable of a nasty cut, especially where children and babies crawl on the floor. In one excavation it was evident that somebody had swept the shards into the corner of the hut where there was a small depression deliberately hollowed to contain them.

If a cluster of huts is found then it suggests that a family or tribal group existed, which adds weight to the theory that the huts were residential rather than storerooms or community buildings. As for the size of a community, it appears that a group of 25 people is necessary to prosper, perhaps four or five families together with their children. The principal need in the building of a hut, as with our beach versions, is timber and this begs the question as to how skilled the Pre-durotriges were at timber construction. On television I watched the Ethiopian Hamar tribe build a hut. Vertical poles of around head height were erected to form a circular wall. The roof was constructed on adjacent ground using light poles to create an upside down umbrella. They then lifted this up, turned it over and carried it to its position over the round walls. Then, sheaves of grass-like vegetation were tied to the roof for the weatherproofing. An elder visiting the hut for the dedication ceremony said "It looks like it was built by a bunch of kids."

In contrast, the archaeological finds at Star Carr in Yorkshire and elsewhere imply that carpentry skills were very advanced in Britain. A wood walkway, now called the "Sweet Track" after its finder Ray Sweet, was built in Somerset in 3800 BC using split oak boards pegged down with hazel and alder. Ladders have also been found with triangular notches cut up a thick wood pole. Lime bast was also used, a skilled process whereby the bark of the lime tree was turned into fibre. This expertize in woodworking is apparent in the mortise and tenon joints on the stone lintels at Stonehenge. This implies that the earlier wood circles looked similar to Stonehenge and had wood lintels across the top of timber posts to form portals or complete wood circles.

With only flint axes, the felling of heavy mature trees just to obtain the lighter upper branches for hut construction sounds improbable. This supports the theory that they were practising coppicing and pollarding, woodland skills available to Europeans because they have suitable tree species. Pollarding usually involves lopping off young oak, ash and lime trees at a height above which cattle and deer can reach. The new growing shoots then form a crown, a circle of branches, and these can be cut from six to fifteen years for use in hut building or fencing. The branches would be given to cattle first, as the bark and leaves are mineral rich and nutritious. The wood stripped of its leaves and not used for construction would be stored as kindling. A pollarded tree does not carry huge branches and rarely falls or blows over. They are also considered to live longer than trees left to grow naturally. The maturing trees create an extensive root system and the re-growth of the crown after pollarding is surprisingly fast, forming long, sound branches. Whether they planted these trees or just utilized self set trees where they grew has yet to be decided.

Coppicing, unlike pollarding, is usually associated with providing small branches for basket making and wattle. Hazel and willow are the primary trees but most British species can be coppiced. It entails cutting the branches off a young tree just above the soil so that a clump, called a stool, develops. A myriad of stems tends to grow vertical and straight from the stool. These can be harvested with a flint axe, conveniently just above ground level at between seven and ten years. This growth only occurs if stock and deer are excluded by fencing as they readily browse such growth. Once their harvesting needs are understood, a rotation of cropping can be developed so that timber is available each and every year for the various tasks. Britain is an ideal place to inhabit if you need timber. Tree pollen found at Bouldner Cliff, off the Isle of Wight, indicates that in 3000 BC the tree species were: pine 15 – 20%, alder 30 – 40%, elm 2%, hazel 35 – 38%, oak 10% and lime (small leaf) which was sporadic.

Where they grew their timber is another consideration. The

pollarded trees can be dotted around water meadows used for grazing and crops because such trees are above browsing height and not in need of protection. Coppicing is more of a problem as ground level stools need to be defended against cattle and deer, which must have been difficult without modern wire fencing. The pine, which readily self seeds, is ideally suited to higher ground such as St Catherine's Hill. It would have given much workable timber but is not a suitable tree for pollarding or coppicing.

Assuming Zuri has the timber, what kind of hut would she aspire to? Perhaps hut design was fixed in stone, so to speak. Did she, like us, endow so much into a property? Would she be so wanting, as we are? The huts Zuri would have known would be to the pattern found by archaeologist Mike Parker Pearson at Durrington Walls. These were five metres square, sometimes with rounded corners. This standard construction would develop a skill set that would ensure that the intensive physical work is kept to a minimum. They would quickly gain an understanding of the timber and the dimensions necessary for a standard hut. The walls were wattle and daub and only locally available material would be used to avoid excessive transportation. Today, we would call this green construction and deem it sustainable and eco-friendly. As I research this topic on the internet Google keeps popping up with "low prices for wattle & daub."

Unlike the gerontocracy Zuri's tribe do not have the resources to make the building anything other than functional. But, would Zuri crave her alternatives to granite worktops and if so, what were they? A decent floor seems high on the list and rammed chalk seems favoured as it offers a hard, clean surface. But, fresh cut chalk is heavy and some way off on the downs, so that can be discounted. Such a floor was found in a building excavated in 2015 at Marden Henge on the upper Avon. The chalk floor is surrounded by what appears to be a chalk bench around the building interior but all the above ground building had rotted away. The floor is as solid today as the day it was laid; patiently waiting to be brushed clean by a birch besom and dare I say it, wielded by a woman.

I needed to see a reconstructed square hut but only round ones existed at Butser Ancient Farm in Hampshire and the Ancient Technology Centre at Cranborne. Only later will square ones be built at Stonehenge Visitor Centre. Round huts appear to be in fashion from the Bronze Age but Zuri would not know these. I found my hut at La Hougue on Jersey. On this site is an impressive chamber tomb and adjacent to it archaeologists had reconstructed a hut based on postholes found nearby. It was rectangular but with no hearth. The builders had underlaid the thatched roof with modern roofing felt. Despite the felt the hut had declined in condition, falling apart in less than a decade. It was a bug hotel, harbouring munching insects, ants and woodlice together with creeping damp and a myriad of fungi. Hazel was used to build the walls and is a favourite woodworm dish. Naively, I concluded that Neolithic tribes must have spent much time and effort refurbishing huts in order to keep them weatherproof but I was to be proved wrong.

I assumed that Zuri's hut had a hearth but no chimney. The evidence in Stone Age communities around the world is that they simply allowed the smoke to seep out through the thatch. This avoided having a hole in the roof through which all heat would escape and rain pour in. It was upon visiting the Ancient Technology Centre in Cranborne that the volunteer staff enlightened me, although walking into the various huts on the site, each with a blazing fire, was all the evidence I needed. Without a roof vent, smoke and fumes build up under the thatch and seep slowly out. This reduces the oxygen level so that any sparks from the fire are extinguished before they reach the highly flammable roof. The smoke also kills the insects and appears to protect the wood. But, this is only true if the fire is burned every day and evidence suggests that such a hut could survive for as long as 40 or 50 years. I was given this information in a reconstructed Iron Age hut, my eyes aware of the blue haze and my lungs slightly distressed but Zuri would have become accustomed to it. As I write I can still recall the cosiness of that fire and the shielded warmth of the hut. The woodsmoke tainted my clothes for many days.

What else did Zuri anticipate in the hut? Beds appear to have been routinely fitted and the Neolithic functionality of a wooden bed can still be researched today. Imagine the baby or child snuggled under a warm cattle skin and having a piddle. The pee runs through the wood poles upon which it lies and drips onto the soil beneath. Some 4000 years later we find the outline of the bed, analyse the soil beneath, find high levels of phosphorus and know that bed wetting was routine. Did they cut a hole in the bed or through any skins they lay upon to facilitate peeing? That would indicate functional creativity. Was it just the children? Perhaps the adults were loath to go outside and so everybody piddled through the poles.

Zuri's people believed, as we do, that they represent the acme of all knowledge. Her hut was well insulated by daub and thatch, the materials being local and the building skills functional. Crucially, the build is quick and the weight light enough not to need sophisticated foundations; everybody can be housed. Only recently, in a nearby street in Friars Cliff, a German factory built house was erected in little more than a week. The biggest pile of construction material was the insulation, the daub as it were. Modern German hut technology seems much closer to Zuri's than to the traditional way that we construct properties in Britain today. Our love of bricks and mortar requires deep foundations, is expensive and so slow that the entire construction is often soaked by rain or frozen in inclement weather.

The German workers, in more than a nod to prehistory, "topped out" the building upon completion by tying a bunch of evergreen branches to the highest point. In the past, we Brits used yew branches for this ritual to ward off evil spirits. I am minded to think that Zuri's hut builders will have done the same but rather than evergreens, did they prefer a deer bone, a shell or even a human skull?

Chapter 13

Pagan Pods

The patriarch took Zuri and Kablea to a location he had identified to build the hut. It was not far from the river yet high and dry, above the dark time floods, looking out over the valley. The patriarch and matriarch were aging and before many moons one of them would die; their hut would lose its spirit. The one who remained would move to another hut, perhaps Zuri's, to where the cooking pots would also be taken. The feeding hearth was the heart of the family. She saw a change in the patriarch, that he could see what was to come and wanted to influence it, to control it. To reflect well upon him and the family the hut had to be built with skill. He set the date for building to begin at the full moon, two moons hence, so that all the materials could be gathered before the work began. He took care to allocate the various tasks to those he considered most suited. There was little squabbling, yet the weight of the work hung over them, adding to their daily tasks. Zuri had never seen a hut built from new. Her family back in the wildwood had patched up their hut for all the moons she could remember but had never built from new. She watched as the patriarch laid claim on timber and as the moons passed, a pile of heavy poles built up. These support timbers were all cut from pine trees, each no higher than required so that axe work was kept to a minimum. The poles were stored beneath an open sided hut to keep them dry. The smell of pine resin grew by each sun. The staves, the uprights for the wattle, and the roof poles, were cut from the hazel coppice where the family harvested their nuts. Zuri had made wattle fencing and knew that if the staves were too thick it was difficult to interweave the wattles. The wattles, the pieces weaved across the staves she selected herself, ensuring they were long, thin and flexible.

She discarded damaged wood as any scarring became rigid and prevented them from flexing. Although she had helped to repair wattle before she was surprised at just how big the timber piles became and how much carrying was involved, and then there was the cutting and drying. She knew that the patriarch would stop them when they had sufficient but that took longer than she expected. The first stave for the walls and the first roof pole was measured against those within their present hut. These would be used as the pattern so that everything would copy what had been done in the past. When they cut new poles and hacked off the small branches, piles of green leaves built up and they had to be carried to the cattle, which ran towards them in anticipation of the feast. She watched them fight over the leaves, aware of all the time the family spent keeping them out of the coppice.

She and Kablea worried that they would not be able to find enough reeds for the roof and suitable daub to fill in the walls. The reeds could only be cut after they had grown over the high sun and there was never enough. The cattle and deer ate them at every opportunity. A thin roof was a leaking roof and she recalled Kablea saying that her people in the wildwood built poor huts. This was because they made a roof with grass or even heather, which were inferior to reeds. The patriarch calmed their anxieties and they understood how wise he was in the building of huts. Moons earlier, he had arranged for branches to be placed around reed beds to prevent cattle from eating them and now they were ready to cut. Other families knew that the reeds were claimed and could not be taken by them. Zuri, while out foraging in the marsh had found reed stands but only in those places most difficult to reach. She waded out to cut them, tying them into bundles before she and the children carried them back. It was dirty work as the reeds were green, wet and slimy. They could not stop until the patriarch judged that there was enough.

The daub was an even greater challenge. Zuri had seen daubed walls built that had fallen down within a few moons. Everybody knew that if sand and silt was used it broke down quickly and demanded constant repair. Clay was needed but it was rare along the river and where it was found everybody wanted it. The patriarch spoke to Nimaz because he knew the clay but it was too far away. It was agreed that they must use riverside mud from where the cattle sometimes drank and this was nearby. It had not the colour of clay but there was a stickiness that meant that it would hold up. Zuri joined the first collection and they each used a bone scapula to shovel the mud into baskets. The mud, full of cattle dung, had been trodden for many moons and stuck to their legs and arms. The baskets were heavy to carry, so little weighed so much and it had to be carried uphill. It was collected every sun and piled into a dip near the hut site where it would dry out, making it easier to mix with the straw and grass that would bind the daub.

When the full moon arrived for construction to begin, the harvest had finished, the grain was stored, the nuts and bearberries collected and only the falling light and cold awaited them. The patriarch watched over the work. The hut base was first levelled, the turf cut from the high side and upturned on the low in order to create a flat area. The pine wall posts were held upright where they would stand and the post holes marked. Each hole was dug tight, smooth and vertical, its depth varying to account for the length of the post so that all the tops were level. The interior posts which supported the roof poles, were higher and had notches cut into them for their feet so that they could climb inside of the roof. The base of each post was charred over a fire to blacken it and prevent it from rotting. Each stood in its hole butted up against the vertical side, the soil being backfilled and rammed so that the posts could not move. Cross pieces were tied around the top linking each post into a rigid square to carry the roof. The roofing poles were lifted up and tied into place supported by the higher ladder posts inside the hut. Poles were cut and tied across the roof poles to form a strong frame, which was steep to help the rain drain off quickly.

The reeding began with sheaves tied around the bottom edge and then working back up the roof. The agile thatchers took turns to sit on the roof, pulling up the bundles of reeds and placing them, each overlapping the one below, spaced so that water ran down reed to reed. Others worked inside tying in the sheaves. The patriarch became agitated, constantly quibbling over this and that; people would mock them if they sat under a leaking roof. The reed at the apex had to be the thickest and with extra binding because if it broke away the entire roof could be ruined. The roof hung over an arm's length out from the walls so that firewood could be dried and stored beneath. When the roof was finished two small yew branches were placed on the top, one for each sister and the shamaness called upon them to protect all who sheltered within it.

The work now focussed on the walls and to prevent them soaking up moisture beams were laid on the ground between the posts. Using a flint axe, sockets were cut into the beams and an upright stave was cut to fit each socket and tied onto the upper frame. The flexible wattles were then interwoven between the staves. The children made play by joining in to make the daub. After water had been fetched in skins it was added to portions of mud, together with dried grass, and the treading began. The mixture had to be just right, smooth yet stiff. They began pressing the daub into the wattles until all the spaces were filled. They worked in pairs on opposite sides of the wall, one person inside and one outside. It took five suns to finish the work and neither legs nor arms were without soreness. It looked to Zuri as if the entire hut had grown upwards from beneath the ground. But she had been told what would happen next, that over the next few suns the daub would dry and crack. More daub, wetter daub, would have to be mixed, the cracks covered and small holes filled to keep out the cold winds.

The hut was to have platforms built against the sides of the walls so that they did not have to sleep on the ground as their forebears had done. Kablea used a pick to cut channels in the floor in which to slot beams for the sides, head and foot. Zuri was able to make up a wattle lattice to fit each platform with just the right tension for sleep. She had already selected stones for the hearth whilst out on her foraging. Flat stones, ones that would take the heat of the fire and continue to warm the hut even after the flames had ebbed. She bedded them into the centre of the hut floor so that they formed a rounded hollow to hold the fire. A store of dried wood was ready, wood for her own fire. She had no cooking pots as the matriarch would continue to cook the food. Only when the matriarch died would that change. With the hearth in place and the sleeping platforms built, the floor could be finished. They brought in baskets of gravel, tipped it on the floor and rammed it with poles. As each spell of ramming ended so she swept the loose material away with birch branches. They rammed and swept until a smooth hard finish was achieved. She then scraped out a small hollow in the corner into which she would sweep flint shards, bone and shell fragments.

As the hut neared completion, people drifted away as other work made demands upon them. Zuri and Kablea still needed somewhere to put tools so that children could not reach them or fall over them. Larger work tools were placed in a deep recess at the end of the platforms. Hand tools, such as pieces of flint, antler and bone, had to be stored in woven hazel baskets and Zuri could make these.

Zuri stood inside the hut, alone, and smelt its newness with its odour of pine resin and reeds. She could imagine herself in the warm times collecting bunches of meadowsweet from near the river and scattering the stems on the floor. The flowers had the scent of the Gods. Yet, the hut was not hers because it belonged to everybody in the family. Now that she had been part of building a hut from new, she was aware of how they changed over many moons. How feet wore a depression at the portal.

How walls were damaged by carelessly dropping tools against the daub. Many times, at the matriarch's hearth she had knelt down fitting her knees into the recesses made when tending the pot on the fire. Yet Zuri's knees would not fit because the hut had moulded itself to the matriarch and become a part of her. Likewise, her cooking pots held her spirit and Zuri felt anxious when she touched them. Each pot was patterned and so many furs and much grain had been bartered for them.

In the new hut Zuri secreted a bone pin, her favourite pin, down between the timbers of the platform. It was a gift to the twin sisters and she implored them to give her their protection. She was weary from the birth and the hut building and still the coughing sickness would not leave her body. She asked the twin sisters to build up her strength for the upcoming journey to the stone circle. At night, her dreams took her to the sunfall ceremony and she was overshadowed by the power of the stone portals.

Chapter 14

Paradise Lost

I have called Avonlands a paradise earlier in this narrative and I need to justify the use of a word which is so often misused. Those golden beaches and hot, dry countries in the holiday brochure are fine for sun lovers but not places where farmers could ever build a future for humanity. Places like Avonlands, that is.

Simon Barnes, the nature writer for *The Times*, put me into this reverie. His version of paradise is "the place where humans are at peace with the rest of creation." His way of reaching this place is to travel to Zambia to find the big five on safari. All I can visualize is declining animal species being harassed by a convoy of jeeps filled with the sunburnt gerontocracy. He emphasises "The whole point of paradise is that it's lost." If paradise is lost then it is because most people have changed their relationship with the land. If true, then this has the potential to demean the way in which we view and understand Avonlands and Christchurch.

The dictionary definition of paradise offers three options. The first is heaven, an imaginary place and probably based on similar imaginary places recalled from prehistoric cultures. The second option is the Garden of Eden, where Adam and Eve resided. The third option is "an ideal or idyllic place or state" and it is this that drives me to describe Avonlands as a paradise. Perhaps a test of this definition is whether I could have applied the word to other places where I have lived, such as South London, Shropshire or Cumbria? The answer is no, as none of them have the same qualities. Zuri's tribe could not have prospered in those places; nobody could until after the Iron Age. Looking to Europe, when Islam created their human paradise in the form of the Alhambra Palace in Southern Spain, it needed copious water, fine soil and lush greenery. These qualities, coming out of the land, the basis of the good life, are the essence of Avonlands.

I would love Simon Barnes to meet Zuri. She knew bears, wolves, perhaps even aurochs and her sea was bountiful with creatures. Unlike Africa, where poor soils abound, she did not need to leave but foraged and grew her way into a successful culture. Some of the wild animals did disappear but was paradise lost? Is it not still about us today, with that essential harmony, for we few, we bungalow dwellers? Surely, if we walk today on Hengistbury Head, ringed by the untamed sea, with Zuri's fertile valley to the north, are we not looking over a paradise? When I walk the undercliff path at Highcliffe, is that goldcrest feeding on the flowering gorse in January any less beautiful than the carmine bee-eater of Africa? Are the mewing gulls not wild enough?

Some might argue that Zuri betrayed nature, as we do, because she dug up the land and tore down the trees, and her people ultimately became too many for paradise to accommodate. Was she aware of this, indeed, could she know that mankind and nature cannot coexist without the one damaging, even destroying, the other?

For me and many in Christchurch, the ground around our property becomes our little paradise, a flowery retreat. My peace, which Simon Barnes suggests you find in paradise, is a mass of tulips, amidst primulas and forget-me-knots. Planted within them is a magnolia, and phormiums from New Zealand clatter in the breeze as grasses from South Africa wave to and fro. It is a typical garden of the gerontocracy, full of the exotic plants which our local nurseries think appeal to us. Their roots are in stony, infertile, heathland soil but as I can afford fertilizers and compost, they grow where they would otherwise perish. I suddenly realize that Zuri wouldn't recognize a single plant in my garden because her heathland is profoundly changed by my wealth, profligacy or ignorance. What does it say about me that

I have a cabbage palm and a date palm growing in my front garden and the neatest lawn edges?

I am guilty because I could have easily and inexpensively maintained my garden as the original heath, a mass of heather and ling, full of bees and insects but chose not to. The garden, it appears, must be an aversion to wildness. When tourists visit Dorset they note the Australian cabbage palms growing everywhere. The gardens at Abbotsbury typify this approach with a frenetic desire to deny the hemispherical location and be called sub-tropical. That exotic mantra dominates the promotional blurb in leaflets about Abbotsbury. It makes Dorset appear warmer so that it will attract rich pensioners to visit and live here. The gerontocracy can save the county because nobody, not least the politicians, has any idea how to move forward now that farming cannot promise us an expanding future.

My garden illustrates how distorted my thinking is compared to Zuri. None of my plants are sustainable because they only grow because of fertilizers and my labour. Without me and my intervention they would succumb to the native species within a few years at most. A consolation is that the garden attracts a myriad of bees and butterflies so all is not lost. It is a composition of petals, leaves, forms and colours that meets my idealized paradise. As with Adam and Eve, without my care it returns to what, up North, they call the waste. The waste in Dorset is the precious heathland destroyed by my bungalow and I am hardly fit to proselytize to Zuri about damaging the environment. Worse, I know better whereas Zuri did not understand that she also reshaped the land and destroyed the primordial forest that grew here as the Ice Age retreated.

Organic gardeners and the Greens are anxious about the way we treat the environment and their definition of paradise would have to include words like sustainable and organic. The English lawn really upsets them because it typically relies upon oil based fertilizer and weedkiller. The gerontocracy, proud of their weed free striped lawn, employ a mass of minions in distinctive overalls, each pushing machines dispensing weed 'n' feed granules. Their vans always display the word green and yet they apply over one million chemical lawn treatments each year. These hirelings rely on soluble horticultural chemicals and their only concession to nature is a prayer to the Gods for rain. Without rain these chemicals fail. This short-termism is endemic. Get somebody else to do the dirty work and keep the conscience untroubled. The firms understand this and employ a fawning marketeer, inspired by those issues that trouble the wealthy aged. Questions and answers are posed on their website. Is the lawn treatment dangerous to children? No. Is the treatment dangerous to pets? No. Is it harmful to the environment? Sorry, my mistake, they don't pose that question as it compromises the product. And don't trouble yourself with what happens when it seeps into the water we subsequently drink. I try to explain to Zuri why wild daises are so threatening in a lawn but she doesn't even understand a lawn; Christchurch didn't have a single lawn in 2200 BC.

Zuri cannot understand how her success in this paradise has resulted in England becoming one of the most densely populated countries in the world. She wants to know where nature has gone and why everything is dominated by people. The beach can hardly be seen, the sea is full of boats, swimmers and boards and the car park packed with vehicles. I cannot tell her that even the sand was out in the bay, under water, just a few weeks ago until we brought it back using mechanical diggers. How could she understand the changes to this piece of land and seashore, which she so coveted? I console myself in the belief that she would find my bungalow and its garden very much to her liking and with M & S and Sainsbury's to sustain me, recognize that it represents a continuation, somewhat distorted perhaps, of her paradise.

Chapter 15

The Fruit of Paradise

The sun warmed the air, the insects buzzed and the butterflies flittered like tiny birds. It had been cool when she went out at first light well before the sun rose and mist cloaked the river. That grey mist disappeared but it was still too early for the birds, the ones that ate the ripe fruit. Zuri was not the only person creeping out of their hut, eager to be first to the harvest. Everybody and everything sought the fruit. On many occasions she had smiled to see the fox, up on his hind legs, using his unwieldy jaws to grab ripe berries. But, the Gods of animals had also given him the fruit. The dark fruit was also the bear's favourite food, which is why it was called bearberry. They fruited after the high sun and were the final sweetness to fatten the bear for the cold times.

When she reached the bramble she picked the bearberries and dropped them into a skin bag. The berry at the tip of the briar was always the biggest, the sweetest and the first to be bagged. Another less ripe berry would take its place and be prime for picking in a few suns. If they did not pick every sun then the over ripe berries would soon turn grey and musty. They would rot, become inedible and wasted. It was finger work and they became so sensitive during the first picking as they tested each berry, too ripe and they tore apart, too unripe and they resisted and had to be left to another sun. It was also dirty and often painful work, the hands and arms pricked all over and left studded with tiny spines. There would be dried blood on the skin with cobwebs and stickiness as the dark juice of the ripe berries stained where it touched. When she picked with other women they would laugh because their arms were always too short. The stretch for the best berries saw them lose their balance and then a long arching briar would clasp them. The spirit of the plant was in the briars and if one spine touched the skin, the whole stem seemed to clasp itself up or down a leg or arm. It was difficult and painful to remove. Zuri knew that the briar did not want to lose its fruit; it would not accept that it was a bounty given by the Gods. The sweetness had to be captured quickly and if they did not eat or cook the fruit before sundown it would spoil. Others were already out collecting crab apples and the bitter fruits would be infused with the bearberries and boiled up to create sweet apple. They looked forward to this all through the warm suns. It was a bountiful time and they no longer had to fear the bears, who loved the berries, as they were rarely seen these days near the river. Yet, they were not forgotten and people would tell stories to frighten the children. And the children saw that people wore bear's teeth or claws around their neck, not just the shaman and shamaness, and the bear claw spoke to them of sweetness tempered by fear.

They ate sweet apple every sun whilst they fruited but the bearberries of this sun were going into the meat stew. The colour, when she saw it in the bowl was an amazing thing to see and the children were fascinated. This was why every family nurtured their own patch of brambles and talked about how they were growing and cropping. Every opportunity was taken to grow more brambles and they even bounded the fields in order to keep cattle inside. The cattle loved the leaves so ate their side of the brambles, leaving the family the fruit on the outside. If the cattle were on both sides they sometimes had fruit only in the middle of the patch. They were all skilled at managing the briar and knew that they could dig one up, choose the place where it would thrive and it never failed to grow.

Zuri coveted bearberry, a gift from the Gods, yet remained puzzled. Why did the plant not grow up in the wildwood on the white soils? She had not known it when she was young. Even down in the valley it was a gift that failed if the briar was not close to water. The Gods would sometimes desert them and a failed crop was a sad time. The Gods needed to make it neither too hot nor too dry to give them full berries. What they needed was warm sun and light rain. She asked the matriarch why the bearberries sometimes failed and she said that the plants had their own Gods so who could know the answer. The matriarch had also shown her how to cut them down just before flowering so that they re-grew, untroubled, and fruited much later. It extended the picking over another moon. Like the bear, many berries would give them succour before the cold and dark times.

Chapter 16

The Joy of Movement

Zuri's people lived shorter lives than we do today and suffered from many of the ailments and diseases that we have overcome. But when we broke our attachment to the land we also eased back on the physical work that this entailed. This has led to an obesity crisis and a media that exhorts us to return to Zuri's time and "exercise like a wild, ancient human."

Without any awareness of fitness, Zuri and her people were light on their feet and moved quickly. The men hunted and tracked wounded animals for many miles whilst the women foraged over wide areas. They both tilled the soil and nobody was still or idle for prolonged periods. With fitness came fecundity, children were born and the population increased. With fitness came acuity, heightened senses and the ability to see and feel their surroundings far more acutely than we can today. They lived as nature intended and when physical movement stopped, they would quickly expire. Zuri, as a forager, is estimated to have walked up to ten kilometres, over six miles every day. She carried loads for much of this distance which would have increased her core strength. It is now proven that as men age they are particularly susceptible to muscle loss and when this happens their general health deteriorates.

All the evidence shows that walking, what we now call the walking cure or green therapy, offers a myriad of benefits beyond muscle tone and heart strength. It increases creative thinking by 60%, strengthens the immune system, lengthens the life of people with diabetes, reduces blood pressure, improves the efficiency of the eyes and cognitive function, improves balance and reduces osteoporosis and cancer of the breast and colon. Another health benefit, not often expressed, is that this muscle tone will increase orgasmic pleasure for women. I am not expert on this subject.

The psychological health of Zuri will have benefited from the motivation and focus inherent in finding and producing food. In recent decades we have also come to realize the mental health benefit of a fit body and exercise is now seen as a form of treatment. On BBC Radio 4 in early 2017 a programme called "Stonehenge and Mental Health" followed a group of Wiltshire residents with mental health issues. Over ten weeks they used Stonehenge as "a human henge," a way to consider how humans then and now cope with life. Interviews with those attending highlighted the need to be outside, which they promoted as ecotherapy or walking therapy. The whole programme was recorded at Stonehenge and throughout, the traffic noise from the A303 intruded. Also, nobody mentioned the impact of air pollution on health.

At over 70 my movement worsens but I am already twice the age of the aged in Zuri's time. I am reminded of my decline every morning by the gerontocracy gymnastics, otherwise known as putting on the pants. It's that movement; stand on the right leg and slip the foot, known to be at the end of the left leg through the hole in the limp cotton pants. It rarely works, the toes, with a life of their own, clasp the seam of the pants and the brain has just enough cognition to recognize that remaining upright, on one leg, is unlikely. Many thousands of us visit A & E each year because of this early morning ritual. I would like to think that as a regular walker I would have the coordination necessary to do this simple movement, but no. As my dotage advances, I have the consolation of a myriad of disability aids to keep me moving, sort of, and Christchurch has the shops with the products for sale. My creaking movement attracts masses of promotional blurb, not least the unsolicited junk mail that streams through the letterbox. It's a half price sale of tri-walkers, bathlifts, stairlifts, wheelchairs, mobility scooters, adjustable beds, riser/recliners and cosyfeet slippers. The marketing whiz that spews out this blurb, perversely, identifies us in a linear decline, beginning our journey as a robust cyclist, one able to power a bicycle. You are then promoted or is it demoted, to an electric bike and when your tyres are finally deflated you flop into a manual wheelchair, followed by a powered wheelchair and then a full-on mobility scooter. It's all perambulatory to disambulatory because nobody tells us that with increasing indolence our body bulk balloons. For people like me who are aging and mobile, yet possessed of aching muscles, this blurb is a constant reminder of my impending frailty on a journey which terminates in a nursing home.

Research now confirms that the moment you cease movement the muscles begin to waste away. The belief that rest is good for us, that it is somehow virtuous, is a misconception. Another misconception is that our buttocks evolved for sitting on. Rest is necessary after extreme exertion and illness but even after surgery the advice is now to be active as soon as possible. The word mobility aligned to the word scooter is an oxymoron.

Muscles are the real organs of pleasure and they require frequent activation. Zuri's muscles were most exerted, not by foraging but by scraping skins, and it created an asymmetrical skeleton, as bones expanded in the arm and shoulder that powered the work. Today, trained athletes might be seen as the equivalent of these ancient exercisers. On average, they will live longer than the slothful but when pushing their body to extremes a few will experience sudden death syndrome; athletes occasionally just drop dead. The body is, after all, a machine and parts fail. Athletes however have the benefit that their exertion releases endorphins which creates a feeling of euphoria; Zuri would have experienced this too.

There is walking and there is walking. The average person walks little and is said to attain three miles per hour. I am sceptical about this. I have noted how people are walking less fast when compared to my younger days. I also occasionally time my walking and if I push the pace I can just exceed four miles per hour. Many people amble, which does not test the body but is better than nothing. The correlation between body weight and walking speed is very strong. Residents of the US walk the least and, consequently, are the most overweight. I would wager that Zuri would match me pace for pace but she would keep going far longer.

Yet walking, what might properly be called hiking in the hilly parts of Britain, is a different thing entirely. In Christchurch, if we see a kitted hiker then we assume him or her to be a coastal path walker and not a local. For good health we are now advised to briskly walk at least three miles each day, a total of 6000 steps. To meet this need, the Christchurch Health Walks are advertised and they promise "Free short walks (45 minutes to one hour). Fitness, fun and good company. Everyone welcome." There is the unwritten expectation of our wonderful walks along the coast, mostly level and blest with lovely views. It is somewhat better than the health walks advertised in Croydon, which take place in the Victorian cemetery; dead good walks you might say.

In considering the walking culture in Christchurch, I walked all the local paths and byways. The walks on the quay and along the leat powering Place Mill are pleasant in themselves but short, and terminate on traffic ridden roads. In Zuri's time this was all marsh and she would have waded through it. A tarmac cycle and walking path from the council offices in Christchurch to Stanpit was inspired planning as it opens the marsh as an extended walking area but there is no traffic free route through to Mudeford. I can walk traffic free from Mudeford and along the coast to Chewton Bunny, where it meets the county boundary with Hampshire. Here, the path turns up the Bunny to a busy road. At this point I met a round Britain walker who, unsure where to go and the tide being in, walked the slumped undercliff down to Barton on Sea and nearly died, up to his thighs in mud.

A safer route will be needed when the proposed round Britain coastal path is finally agreed.

Having put these coastal paths to east and west of Christchurch to one side, there was only one significant walk heading inland. This was promisingly signposted 'the Avon Valley Path' and follows the Avon left bank through a hotchpotch of industrial sites to Knapp Mill and then over the water meadows to spend much of its length crossing or beside busy roads. It is not relaxed walking or good hiking. This lack of decent footpaths reflects how public expenditure is still lavished on the road network with little allocated to expanding the walker's horizons. Consequently, in Christchurch few people really walk.

In Zuri's time it is estimated that there were ten people per 100 square kilometres. The current figure is 42,000. Most experts contend that this was insufficient people to create and maintain paths in all but the immediate home locality. Footpaths soon grow over if not walked frequently. I well imagine a good path will have followed the river because the people lived along the valley. Although the farmers cut back into the woodland to clear areas to graze cattle and goats, the footpaths would only service those areas. Up north they call this land the intake. Beyond that, the dark forest would have dominated and would, in most cases, be impenetrable to all but the seasoned hunter and forager. Even today, if as a walker, you leave the Avon, you quickly find the trees blend together to somehow flatten the horizon and make it indistinct. It is soon impossible to know where you are as few heights exist. Follow the river or become lost remains the rule, as much today as in Zuri's time.

Chapter 17

The Avon Legacy

"Are you happy with your smile?" It was a question on the dentist's medical questionnaire. The dental focus had morphed into some psychological marketing reliant on creating dissatisfaction with my physiognomy. Zuri was as puzzled as me over what an unhappy smile would look like. I decided not to remind her that dental decay was endemic in her tribe, with tooth loss as well as many acutely painful, pus filled abscesses, forming a cavity in the jaw. She did not realize that their diet was creating masses of bacteria around their teeth. The nuts, acorns and certain plant foods did not help but as farming developed, grain porridge and bread made matters worse. Experts suggest that their teeth often killed them.

I am aware that I could never know what ailments Zuri suffered from or why her tribe lived such short lives. I hoped to gain an insight when I visited the museum in the Hodgkin Building at King's College, London. After a brief introduction, Ann and I were let loose amongst the exhibits, thousands of body parts sitting on shelves on three levels surrounding an open atrium. We could pick up many of the exhibits, study them and refer to a folder explaining why they had been retained. Massive neck goitres due to iodine deficiency, deformed limbs and foetuses, tumours, axe damage on various skulls, babies subjected to infanticide and life changing skin infections, all were insights into the past. The scale of human frailty was overwhelming. Yet, no matter how informative and useful the exhibits, it was the postmortem that led to the greatest medical and surgical advances.

Our tour of King's College included the mortuary, where naive 18-year-old medical students assembled to dissect their first cadaver. Using a scalpel, they cut into real flesh, layer by layer. If you ever need an operation these are the surgeons you want. Those who only train on a dummy, or through books and computer graphics, are known to be inferior.

Each body was dissected and examined over three years. What remained was then sent for cremation and the ashes returned to the family. The death might have been lamented yet the body is reinvigorated as a gift to medical science and humanity. What became apparent was that religious dogma skewed the donation of the bodies. The issue is that the dissected body no longer looks like a body. This offends those who believe that our mortal remains should not be violated before they return to their maker. Consequently, adherents of the Catholic, Jewish and Islamic faiths are poor at gifting. Nobody was saying but it struck me that the majority of donations must come from agnostics, atheists, communists and anarchists and those of the pragmatic Church of England; people who see medical science as their God. Members of the gerontocracy, that crotchety old man and woman at the checkout in Sainsbury's are able to ignore centuries of ritual, of religious damnation and surrender their corpse to the greater good. An afterlife that demands an intact body has consequences.

King's College need bodies yet they are fussy. The obese, the anorexic, those experiencing a recent operation, dementia or having had a postmortem, are not wanted. Age does not matter provided they are over 17-years-old, but they are still unwanted if organs had been donated, other than cornea. How would Zuri have responded? Would she have demanded that her corpse be passed to the underworld in its complete state? Zuri and I will tell you more about this later.

Zuri knows that life is dangerous yet she does not understand the real threat, that of harmful and unseen microbes. She would have little understanding that food poisoning and disease could be prevented by cleanliness and good hygiene. It was difficult to keep clean in their environment, not least because they were handling and gutting fish and animals on a daily basis. All the skeletons we have from that period, which is not many, suggest that few people lived to a good age. A number had experienced serious bone injury, yet these had often healed and not caused their death. Everyday cuts, stings and minor injuries must have become infected with the risk of septicaemia and death.

Perhaps age, based on time, was a meaningless concept. There is no evidence that they celebrated birthdays because they could not record them. The limited data we have suggests that Neolithic men lived an average 33.1 years and women 29.2 years, but treat those figures with care. The reality was that age would have been measured by milestones in life. What a person contributed to the tribe mattered and perhaps all older people were given greater status than today because of their time served knowledge and skills. At times, age was a state, and the first period changed a girl into a woman who could bear children. As I write this, the BBC is interviewing four people in a care home, all over 100 years-of-age. The interviewer asks them the secret of longevity but there are no revelations. Always look forward, forget the bad things and recall only the good, is the gist of it. As for old age in our society, when George Melly was asked, "Who wants to live to the age of 99?" "Those who are 98," was his reply.

Zuri's society faced a short, vibrant, fecund, pagan life, one in which the individual played a key role. They would not have experienced a period of morbidity, as we do now. This is our latter years prior to death where the quality of life is poor and a return to good health unachievable. Then there is the issue of being discounted by society, of loneliness and being seen as little more than a pension and NHS liability. As we age, our children age and pensioner parents are now being cared for by their pensioner children.

A major threat to Zuri's people was tuberculosis, often

called consumption. It is thought to have moved from cattle into humans at some time in the Neolithic, after we stopped being hunter-gatherers and domesticated cattle. Such diseases are called zoonotic and include influenza. The irony is that health-giving milk infected us with Mycobacterium bovis and introduced an infectious disease that has killed more humans than all other diseases and plagues put together. Although we do not have natural immunity against TB, those who recover from a mild strain develop antibodies. Neolithic people also lived close together, coughing in the hazy smoke of the fire, lulled into a false sense of security by the odour of burning wood and the glowing warmth. Worse, we now appreciate that woodsmoke is carcinogenic and it also leads to emphysema and bronchitis. The hut ensured that they had a daily dose of smoke; comfort, cancer and consumption were their hutmates. Recently, TB has increased in Britain, and worldwide killed 239,000 children under the age of 15 years in 2015.

Zuri's people would also have been infested with intestinal parasites. Two forms of roundworm can be anticipated, probably whipworm, Trichuris trichiura, and giant roundworm, Ascaris lumbricoides. Up to a third of the world's population still carry these parasites due to poor hygiene although some people with the necessary antibodies are resistant. The symptoms might have gone unnoticed, particularly if everybody had them. These would include low body weight, a poor supply of breast milk and underdeveloped children. Otzi, the iceman found in the Alps, was carrying whipworm. Bizarrely, some people now deliberately infect themselves with worms as a means of reducing their weight. What is still not understood is whether specific intestinal worms might offer some health benefits. Their waste, including faeces, is released into our gut microbiome and it may provide enzymes or chemicals that benefit us. This would be an example of symbiosis and similar symbiotic relationships exist all over the natural world. Unfortunately, the downside is that worms in humans appear to aggravate and worsen iron deficiency anaemia.

However, there was an element of Zuri's environment that would have benefitted her health. Calcium is essential for healthy bones and teeth and the River Avon, particularly above Ringwood, has perhaps the highest level of calcium in any river in the world, at 320 milligrams per litre. Downriver this drops to 270 milligrams but even this level provides at least 50% of our daily calcium requirement. It's those wonderful springs and winterbournes, which Zuri's tribe venerated, where silvery pristine water burbles up full of calcium carbonate from the chalk. This is also the scale which quickly forms in our kettles in this locality. Away from the chalk and limestone, soft water in the UK can be as low as 10 milligrams per litre, thirty times less.

Zuri did not realize that she lived in a calcium dietary paradise, where the water was complimented by the calcium in the fish and milk they routinely consumed. Their infants, relatively, will have thrived. This is the Avon legacy, a wonder, perhaps widely known in the Neolithic. They would have come to realize that a fractured bone in this locality would heal much better than elsewhere. Zuri's tribe didn't know of calcium so they would have ascribed this healing to the Gods. Did Stonehenge become the prehistoric Lourdes, the calcium circle? At Salisbury Museum you can marvel at the strong skeletons on display with fractures healed by new bone.

Zuri's people were not completely helpless in the face of illness. For thousands of years they had eaten plants and knew that some of these had healing qualities. Trial and error came into it and even poisonous plants and fungi, in moderation, do not kill and might just cure. Today, watercress is thought to have been an ancient treatment for tuberculosis and it would have been common in local streams in spring and early summer. They may have eaten large quantities, either cooked or uncooked. It would certainly have raised their iron level. Plants like wormwood and ramsons (wild garlic) may have been eaten and it would have removed all or the majority of their gut worms. This reliance on medicinal plants continued through herbalists in medieval times and still exists today. We have to bear in mind that many of the diseases which killed Zuri's people were not uncommon right through to the end of the 1940s, when antibiotics became the game changer.

Zuri's people did not understand how the body worked although in eviscerating deer and other animals, they would have realized how similar our bodies were. Lung tissue, for instance, looks the same and is linked to the mouth and breathing, and coughing would be readily associated with the chest. This is why a lichen called tree lungwort, which looks like lung tissue, was used to treat lung disorders, at least from medieval times. Would Zuri believe that the Gods were guiding them by creating plants that had similarities to what they were treating? Alternatively, perhaps they just remembered plants by relating them to things they knew and saw. Due to air pollution lungwort is now rare in Britain. The use of wort in plant names implies a history related to medicinal use.

We need to return to the gut and the unsexy subject of constipation, which so many people today do not take seriously. I doubt that Zuri experienced constipation with her plant based diet, ample water and an active lifestyle, all of which keep the gut moving. Conversely, many consider constipation the curse of the gerontocracy. Perhaps this is why Christchurch has three health food shops, as the gerontocracy try to avoid ailments of the bowel. The irony is that here we are, using our money to buy expensive spelt wheat, nuts and seeds to replicate Zuri's diet in order to defecate naturally. Both Zuri and I smiled when *The Times Magazine* outlined the latest fad, the SIRT diet and stated that we should "Eat like a wild, ancient human."

The reality is that our good health and longevity has been attributed more to improved hygiene, clean drinking water and better housing rather than to the impact of medicine or diet. Flushing toilets and clean fingers have much to commend them. Before we get a little smug, our longevity brings new anxieties with increasing levels of dementia and cancer.

Zuri and her people would have a distinctive body odour but I hesitate to call it unpleasant. They had no soap, no deodorants and no appreciation that such products could be necessary. I recall meeting the Masai in Tanzania and they had a very distinctive body odour. Other members of our group blamed this on their practice of piercing the blood vessel of a cow and draining off fresh blood to drink. Our East African guides laughed at this because they said that the Masai found our European odour somewhat strong and blamed it on us eating so much dairy produce. Zuri and her people may also have drunk fresh cattle blood, a rich nutrient source that avoids killing the animal. But, unlike the Masai, she lived in a watery world. Her people would have been in and out of salt and fresh water in their daily foraging, and so were relatively clean by Neolithic standards. This was, potentially, a considerable health advantage for riverine people.

As our knowledge of Zuri's tribe is poor, it can be useful to consider wider research carried out on what remained of Stone Age people around the world. It can, at the very least, offer us an insight into their world. In the Central Library in Cape Town, South Africa, they had an exhibition about a seven-year-old Namibian boy, whose hunter-gatherer father was killed when the child was abducted and sold into slavery. He ended up in the Victorian Cape Town home of the English linguist Lucy Lloyd, who interviewed him in great detail about his childhood and wrote up 17 notebooks. Although he had led, by our standards, a life of deprivation, he had been happy. Moreover, he proved to be highly skilled, even at the age of seven, in the recognition and use of plants and animals.

He was most likely a San, the indigenous and peaceful people of South Africa. They were ultimately wiped out by the tribes of herders moving down from the north 2000 years ago, as well as by the Dutch and English after 1700. Hunter-gatherers were despised by "advanced" peoples, not least by those tribes who had adopted the farming life.

I subsequently visited Nelson Cave on the Robberg Peninsular, south of Cape Town. The excavations there showed that Africa had no Copper, Bronze or Iron Age; that the Stone Age continued right through to the 1700s, when Dutch sailors arrived. The Stone Age ended just 300 years ago. In truth it must have lasted much longer as European metal tools were probably not universal in Africa until the Victorian age. What leaps out is that the poor soil and grazing, unnavigable rivers, absence of native cattle and the parched summers, with wildfires, kept the San on the margins. They were small people and, it appears, suffered much ill health. Surplus food was not an option and without it they were never to build a Stonehenge.

Relatively speaking Zuri is in good health but all the evidence suggests that her people increased slowly in numbers. This tells us that her period of fertility probably lasted no more than ten years. Each woman had to manage the survival of just over two children, on average, to an age when they could reproduce. Her health issues may well have caused her to overdose on the natural remedies they used, many of which were poisonous when used to excess. This could have caused her to spontaneously abort on a number of occasions. Unlike us, Zuri would not separate medicine and religion into two distinct topics. For her, they were unified and subject only to the dispassionate Gods.

Chapter 18

The Nature of Acquisition

It struck me that Zuri would be very comfortable in my kitchen with its new Stone Age work surfaces. Any anxiety is all mine. I recall looking at massive slabs of the black granite at the suppliers and feeling overwhelmed by guilt, that all this weight had been shipped from Brazil. Yet, I was allured by the glossy finish, the quartz having formed white streaks over millions of years, like gas clouds obscuring the blackness of space. The marketeer had similar inspiration and had named it Black Cosmic. I knew that Zuri would be impressed when I told her that I had a cosmos imbued into the kitchen. To fit that kitchen, an unnecessary acquisition, the existing kitchen was disposed of, partly through eBay.

When it comes to waste, the world must fear me. If my lifetime cast-offs were heaped outside my bungalow, as Zuri's midden was outside her hut, it would comprise a mound the size of Silbury Hill. Imagine, the cars, the tyres, bicycles, entire kitchens, bathrooms, wardrobes, tools and mowers, all those newspapers, tins, and that unspeakable plastic. Okay, I have always recycled but that is hardly the point. As gerontocracy, I can afford to have the waste removed and somebody else to sort it, hopefully without detriment to their environment. Nobody will be able to identify me in a few thousand years by my acquisitions, as they appear from my waste heap. Fortunately, we can do this with Zuri.

I should, and I do, try to reduce my waste. Loath to buy anything, I still perambulated around the gerontocracy storeroom, otherwise called John Lewis. Ann said to me, "Is there anything you want whilst we are here?" I could answer, no, absolutely nothing. In that comment I shrugged off two extensive levels of household stuff, tens of thousands of products for sale, from all over the globe. I put on my smug face but who am I kidding?

Zuri's midden, her waste heap, is fulfilment for the archaeologist, containing flint, as well as pottery and, in our area, some bones. The wood hafts, the handles, and other organic waste will have rotted away and no longer exist. But what is evident is how little she threw away. Flint could be re-knapped into ever smaller useful tools, and even wood and skins must have been reused to some degree and perhaps burnt as a last resource. Zuri's carbon footprint was rock bottom.

This begs the question as to why, compared to her, we are so acquisitive, that we need stuff. Perhaps USA writer Paul Shepard, who wrote on evolutionary theory, provides the answer. He stated that humans have spent 99% of their social history in hunting and gathering. Now we are divorced from nature, he postulated, modern humans do not fully mature, remaining infantile and adolescent. It appears that people choose partners for reasons other than their utility and generations later, nobody grows up. This comment reminds us about how Zuri reaches maturity at a very early age. She is utility itself, her body a baby machine, to which we can add her foraging skills and her ability to handcraft various products. Her life skills, which possess so much value, are why she was taken into a farming family.

Media reports seem to agree with Paul Shepard's analysis. The BBC, reviewing UK business, stated that 2000 studios now create video games for sale. They asked the owner of one of these firms what his games were about and he replied "Mostly cars, going fast!" A second report in *The Times* stated that 43% of women between the ages of 18 and 49 have never married. It appears that these women consistently complain that they cannot find a man with a sense of maturity. In the same paper, a former Dean of Stanford University in North America is highlighting the hopeless teens, the sheltered girls who telephone their mother every day from their new college and have no life skills.

Zuri's people made things and left them for us to find. This was part of a linear development in acquisition. The hunter-gatherers were closest to nature and yet had the least amount of stuff. The little they left us were mostly utility items such as arrow heads and flint scrapers. By Zuri's time, when farming was developing, acquisitions such as ceremonial mace heads and what we might call jewellery begin to appear. Metal, the ultimate acquisition, will later change society and influence the way we act today.

I imagine Zuri, contemptible of us all, being bartered and sent away from home, a virtual breeding machine with no understanding of sex, a body traded in exchange for food and security, for her and for her parents. Zuri, like the San boy in Africa, would be treated more like a small adult and less like a child.

Zuri must have played with work from the moment she could walk. The parents had to make the best use of their children in order for the family group to survive. This is not the same as the way we exploited children in Victorian cotton mills. As a child in the wildwood, she would quickly learn the simplest foraging skills like collecting nuts, crab apples and common plants. After a short time she would do this alone or with other children. This would release the adults to do the more specialized tasks. Some tasks needed the dexterity of tiny hands and fingers. At first, these might have been fashioning small balls of local chalk, acorns or snail shells, piercing and stringing them to make a necklace. As they became stronger and more skilled, they would use teeth or bone from the foot, hand or spine of small animals. The really skilled would use chunks of Kimmeridge Shale traded on the river, breaking and polishing this stone into two–three millimetre beads and piercing them with a flint drill tip. Shells such as periwinkle must have been traded up the river as sea shells are often found inland in depositions of charcoal.

Bear, boar and deer bones also held a fascination in that period. Women appear to have used adornment, perhaps for fertility, in the Mesolithic period, prior to 3000 BC, with bird bones used for simple bead necklaces. These are found under the North Sea in what we now call Doggerlands, an area frequented by hunter-gatherers before the melting glaciers raised sea levels.

Zuri's skills and her ability to bear a child would have set her position in society, a position not based entirely on her gender. Women from her time onwards appear to experience a decline in status as society changes when metal becomes a commodity. The archaeological evidence suggests that in the subsequent Bronze Age, when copper, bronze, amber and gold were tooled, men took over the specialized roles of producing these laborious and complex items. That possibly also extended to pottery, earlier considered a woman's skill but less so as pottery became more decorated in what we call the Beaker period. For certain, sophisticated weapons, the metal tools of war, will appear in greater numbers as the warrior culture further diminishes the role and status of women.

Was Zuri a maker of tools? She was born into a hunter-gatherer family and they would have made their own bows and arrows and needed woodworking skills. None of the biodegradable content has survived and it is an assumption that they used yew for bows and ash for arrow shafts. The earliest flint arrowheads were pointed and chunky. They became much finer as their design changed over the centuries. Some are so delicately worked that they might never have been intended for actual firing, but were either a status symbol or had spiritual value.

Although little archaeological excavation has occurred in Christchurch, there are an extraordinary number of stone axes in the Red House Museum. Most came from the area around the railway station. The artefacts found on Hengistbury Head indicate that trading was extensive, with some stone axes from

Cornwall and a few from the Langdale "axe factory" in the Lake District of Cumbria. It appears that Cornish greenstone is the most common material. The source of flint is rarely identified, yet we know that high quality flint nodules were traded around the country from places like Grimes Graves, in Norfolk. I refer to this as the black flint.

We have no way of ascertaining where these tools were made. This might have been wherever the material was sourced or they might have been imported into Christchurch as roughouts and then worked into tools. It could be assumed that the physical effort in making them demanded masculine input. That does not appear the case, as the flint required rather more skill than force. Even the stone axes, assuming they were imported as rough tools, needed polishing using a harder stone. This required many hours of unrelenting tedious work and could have been done by either a woman or a man.

The hours spent polishing stone impacted upon me when I handled a Neolithic mace. This was on the island of St Martin's on the Isles of Scilly in a field looking south mere metres from the sea. The extensive excavation site was a mass of bare soil with many post holes and the odd assemblage of stones. The mace had been excavated only the day before, its assumed wood haft having rotted away. An expert on Neolithic skills was present and he demonstrated how the hole might have been drilled through the mace head. The drill was a piece of wood similar to a broom handle. A shell, pierced with a hole large enough to hold the tip of the wood, was held in place on the mace. This directed the wood to where the hole had to be ground out. Sand was the grinding material put under the tip of the wood. A leather or sinew bow was then used to spin the wood shaft back and fore, repeatedly grinding the sand under its tip. He considered it a two man job taking many weeks. The mace I handled had a perfect round hole as if it had been machine cut. It did not occur to the expert that women might have done this work.

It is considered that women foraged for 66% of all their food and the men would have spent the time when they were not hunting or farming, making and repairing tools. Some research suggests that, when making antler tools, the deer's left antler was preferred by the majority, those who were right handed. Perhaps even the handle on this antler was shaped to fit a right hand, showing further refinement.

What is not understood is the spiritual or symbolic value of the tool or the material used to make it. There clearly was some form of power in stone, perhaps even in antler, and it is possible that tool manufacture had a shamanistic aspect to it. To support this theory, tools were deposited in pits or ditches by Zuri's people after being deliberately broken.

As for pottery, the earliest found is called Windmill Hill Ware, named after the hill above Avebury, Wiltshire. These are crude round pots with no decoration, all fired in an open fire, as they had not invented kilns. Later, they created what we now call Peterborough Ware, with extensive decoration, sometimes using fingernail or finger indentations as a form of decoration. Grooved Ware then appeared and was more widespread throughout the UK, as if somebody, nationally, had devised the shape and intricate basket patterns around the outside of the pot. Some of this has been found in Christchurch Harbour. It appears to be a well traded though fragile item, perhaps made in the Orkney Islands and shipped around the coast. Finally, the Beaker People arrived (more about them later) and we can measure time by the small clay "Beaker" pots, each built up with coils of clay, moulded by hand. The beaker itself appears to be a drinking vessel for some form of alcohol, perhaps emblematic of an increasingly male or warrior dominated society. Would Zuri have lusted after Grooved Ware? Why should she be any different to us? Her Neolithic economy operated on pottery, flint, furs and antler, all high value, functional items and yet constantly evolving.

Zuri and Kablea are preparing to go to Stonehenge and craft their tools and other items in readiness. They remain ignorant that there they will experience perhaps the most significant event in the first 8000 years of this country's history. They will see their first metal, unaware that the communal life is doomed, as status through ownership will change society. Acquisition will take on a new significance which will expand to the present times. In the 1970s, newly married and resident in distant Wolverhampton, I bought pottery from Dorset, even more decorated and heavily marketed. This was a Poole Pottery dinner service called Springtime and I was unaware that its heritage stretched back to Avonlands.

Chapter 19

Flint 'n' Bone 'n' Stone

Zuri had been called a bone crafter from her earliest days and it gave her great pride. She could recall the joy of handling and using bone even when she stood no higher than the dogs, the same dogs that would steal and gnaw the bone. Her mother had always given her the hands and feet of squirrels, foxes, badgers and every small creature that existed; nothing would be wasted. The animals had been snared and occasionally found dead. She knew how to use a small, sharp flint, to tease off the skin and tendons and separate the hand or foot into bundles of tiny, matching bones. She would prize these, collecting them together until she had enough to make a necklet. But she could not keep them too long because fresh bone was best for crafting and as it saw out suns it became brittle and less easy to work. She selected them so that they hung well around the neck or wrist. People admired her work and it would be bartered for other goods. Her mother would constantly tell people how good she was at this task. As a child, she made necklets, sun after sun. As she grew older she was needed to forage in the warmer times or carry kills, so the bone work was restricted to when it was colder or the weather wild.

Bone crafting was demanding, and it needed her small hands and all her attention. She would squat outside, from sunup to sundown, aware that her deft fingers were reforming the hands of the squirrel, the little animal that clawed its way up and down trees. Sometimes, she used the fur tuft of their little red ears, as the central feature of the necklet. Having collected and matched the bones, she had to decide how to drill them and hang them. Did she want to drill the bone down its length and create a snake of bone, or drill through the top and have the bones dangle freely around the neck, like loose feathers? Anybody could hang bones but to hang them well was much more difficult. The cutting of the hole through the bone was intricate and she had to select a tiny flint to bore it out. The bone had to be soaked in water first, to soften it, the bigger pieces for some suns. It dried out quickly so had to be wetted whilst she worked. Her fingers would often bleed, both from holding and spinning the flint and because the flint would snap, breaking into slivers and sometimes cutting into her skin. Yet, she was deft with flint, always able to select the right piece, and she could even knap larger pieces into blades that were just right for her small fingers. Her mother noted this and used other children to collect firewood or water so that she could be left to create necklets.

As she grew, she had strung the bone using her own hair, growing it long so that she could cut and plait it for use as cord. When the necklet was complete, she washed it using soapwort and that made the hair shine. It shone like the black flint, which was from far away and needed more barter than they could provide. The family had to use the poorer local flint dug from pits on the white rock hills. These flints were found as large, flat, gnarly stones, as big as her head and were often too heavy for her to pick up and she had to call for help. These could be bartered down the valley because, with no white rock by the river, they were unable to find nodules. Although poor compared to the black flint and having a lower barter, it made much better cutting and scraping tools than the small flint pieces found scattered over beaches and along the cliffs.

Digging up flint nodules was heavy work but as children they were good at scratting away the white rock until they located them. This left her parents free to do other work. Each nodule had to be carried back to the hut, washed and stored. When they wanted new flint, her father would select a nodule, place it upon the ground and then say words to the Gods. Only when she was taller than the dogs, did she understand why her father thanked the Gods of the underworld for the gift of flint, and why he asked for it to be good flint so that it would sustain them. He would then use a hammerstone, a sacred one that that had been used by their forebears, to strike the nodule and open it for the first time. It had to be struck just right, so that the blow cracked it open and the flint shattered into flakes. This was done over an old, stretched skin, so that all the pieces were collected, otherwise, slivers would shoot away and some might lie about to cut their feet. They would carefully sort the flakes, putting aside the large ones that might later be knapped into axe heads and other hand tools. The smaller ones were then sorted, some for arrowheads, and others to be used as scrapers or cutters. Zuri would be given the smallest and they were her special tools, selected for her little hands. Sometimes, the flint was poor and the nodule would break up into awkward pieces, as if the Gods had not heeded her father's invocation. When this happened, her father would talk of the black flint, how much better this was to knap, and how sharp the edges were. He would never curse the flint; it was a gift from the Gods, whether good or bad. He had always told her that if she used the flint well then it would not snap.

Now that her hands were too large to make necklets, she often made pins using the bone from bird wings. They were light and easily ground away with a piece of stone to a smooth finish. Because they were fine they broke easily or were lost and replacements were always needed. That was her present work, as they all made ready for the journey to Stonehenge. Skins had to be prepared or repaired and the pins made to hold them in place.

What Zuri really liked to work on was antler but very little of this reached her hands. If antler picks snapped, the men used the broken pieces to make other tools. Only rarely did small pieces get passed down to her and these polished much smoother than bone. Kablea had all the antler. From this, he crafted picks, drilling a hole and fitting a wooden haft. They were the tools that he was to use at Stonehenge. The farmers were growing in numbers and antler was becoming the most precious barter along the river. Everybody needed it and yet the farmers had to kill the deer along the river to stop them eating their crops, so antlers became fewer and fewer. When Kablea went hunting in the dark times he had to travel further into the great forest to find the deer. This made her realize that her father, back in the wildwood, had so many skills, often the skill of the eye. He watched and knew so many things. He knew deer better than he knew people. He knew their land; that these animals had a homeland, just like people, and as the dark times ended the stags would go to the same place to shed their antlers. He waited until the frogs spawned in the pool and out he went, often with the children, locating these places and sometimes they returned with armfuls of antlers. They brought joy to the family, as they could barter them for food and other needs. But, the Gods tested them and sometimes the antlers could not be found because other hunters had got there first.

Her father told her that the Gods gifted the antlers to them and so the Gods demanded that they protect the deer. That meant driving the wolves away. Their cunning, he would say, was to watch the stags fighting and when they were enfeebled they would move in for the kill. He trapped and killed the wolves, yet he used their skins and bodies with care, aware that the Gods gave the wolf much strength. They were the only animal who could outlast the pursuing hunters, sun after sun. Yet, her father too showed cunning, because he knew that although the deer slept and sheltered in the forest they liked to feed on the plants in the open meadows. He and the other hunters made clearings in the trees for the plants that liked the sun, and the deer came to them. The lure of the plants was stronger than their fear of the hunters. The antlers they most desired were on the heads of the big red deer, those of the fighting stags, grimed in sweat and blood. They even protected these stags after they were beaten and could no longer fight over the hinds. Old stags had the biggest antlers but, after a few sunfalls, the antlers would become smaller. The old stags were blind to this, that their antlers no longer protected them and their meat was fit for the pot, along with that of the hinds. Yet caring for the deer and their antlers caused so much strife. Other hunters from beyond the wildwood would come to kill animals and take the antlers that belonged to Zuri's people.

Kablea was occupied making his tools for the work he would be doing at Stonehenge. He had to craft spare antler picks because it was so easy to break the points. Picking was a two man operation, one holding the pick in place as the second struck it with a hammerstone, forcing the point into the white rock so that small chunks were eased out, one after another. Kablea would soon leave for Stonehenge and a moon later, Zuri and the baby would follow with others. He waited for the shaman to tell him when to join his group, and head upriver. The shaman knew what work was planned, and the lower river families, which included Kablea, would be reconstructing the ditch and bank either side of the avenue to Stonehenge. It would all be work using his antler picks to break up the white rock in the ditches, putting it into baskets and tipping it over the old banks. The banks would be white and glisten and form the line of approach to the circle. There would be rivalry between different groups to build their section first and reach the agreed junction points before others. This would show the Gods their dedication; the first would be favoured.

The men, with their tools, also had to herd a bullock, a milch cow and pigs, to Stonehenge. Those from other areas would also herd animals and all these people would gather in the work camp, where they would dwell whilst carrying out the work, and then stay on for the sunfall ceremony. There would be no time to hunt or forage for food, so the meat and milk walked there and other food would be taken by river. When they arrived, they would have to repair the huts first, because they would remain at the camp for at least one moon.

Fish, smoked fish, was needed and for many suns before the journey, the sea fish they caught were hung up inside the smoke hut. If the Gods were with them they would catch the red fleshed fish as it ran the river. These were so thick that they had to be sliced into strips before being smoked. The smoke from the fish seeped through the reeds of the roof and drifted around the huts. It was as if the smell told them that the sunfall ceremony was approaching. The smoked fish, together with nuts, grain and crab apples was sealed into a log boat and paddled up the river, the paddlers keeping in contact with those herding the beasts along the riverbank.

Zuri was excited at the thought of the ceremony and how she would retell it again and again upon her return. She and her baby would have their own ceremony at the great circle where the shamans would attend only the bearers; she would be one of them.

Chapter 20

To the Temple

I looked across to where Zuri slept in the work camp, perhaps 100 metres from where I am parked at Durrington Walls. I make no noise, somebody, I suspect, is sleeping in a van only a few metres from me. I had anticipated having to walk in the dark and had brought a torch but I am surprised at how the light crept in at least an hour before sunrise. It sidled in from below the southern horizon whilst the north remained quite dark. Venus, a glowing planet low in the sky was quickly obliterated by the brightness yet I knew that it was still there. Zuri knew the planet by another name. As I walked away from Durrington Walls, across the field and past the cuckoo stone, the guttural carrion crows woke the world. Each lifelong pair was warning other black couples that this was their zone, their patch, just as they had done to Zuri and her people 4000 years earlier. That was before modernity had lit up the horizon with a mass of orange sodium and red navigation lights for those flying in and out of Boscombe Down airfield.

My inadequate trainers slewed about on the wet grass and chalky mud and moving quickly, I turned left across the foot of the Greater Cursus and passed the Bronze Age tombs crowning King Barrow Ridge. Then I turned right through a gate into a grass field. There were no ancient indentations but I knew that I had stepped onto the avenue, the ceremonial way to the great Temple that Kablea had refashioned with his antler picks. I was also standing in Zuri's footsteps or rather, above her footsteps, which lie unexcavated beneath my feet. She had walked up from behind me on what is now private farmland leading back across the A303 and down to the River Avon. I, or is it we, were about half way along the avenue, which extends for 1.7 miles between the river and Stonehenge.

Unlike last summer, there was no bull with his harem or any sheep in the field so no cowpats or curranty poo. Neither was there a human in sight. My now wet feet preceded my dulled brain as it caught up with an acute observation that every single blade of grass terminated in a globule of water. This droop of crystal water was the accumulated humidity from the chill air. Reflected in the globules I am shocked to see daisy flowers, fresh as a daisy, even though it was the 23 December 2015. It was the mildest winter ever recorded yet we have recorded a mere 1% of the 10,000 years people have stood in this field. With the half light coming in from my left, the tussocks of grass to my right stretch out like dull pillows strewn across the broad downs, a virtual organic eiderdown. To the west, a pile of stones rear up and try to mimic a circular Temple but fail in the poor light. I am aware that my modern eyes in this light are weak and that at this point, Zuri, with her night vision rods, would have seen the Temple more clearly than I ever could. Though made of large stones it looks so small set in this wide, flat landscape. Zuri would see a Temple built of white stone, the virgin stone, newly hammered to display its pristine whiteness. I am looking at grey stone: correction, I am not looking at stone at all. I am looking at the veneer of lichen and algae mosaic plastered all over the stone by 4000 years of nature. Bare stone is rare, except where the air is polluted and lichen and algae cannot grow. All this science is unknown to Zuri. My vocabulary is not hers. The English language too, is deficient. The Celtic word 'cynefin', which describes the environment to which you are accustomed, its shared history, has no English equivalent.

I walk on rapidly, knowing the precise though unmarked route down into the shallow valley, which sees the Temple mass disappear behind the slope. Why does the avenue bend and dip so that on the approach the stones appear, then disappear and then reappear?

Through another gate and staying with the bend it's as if

the avenue will miss the Temple by some distance but then the conundrum. The ceremonial way suddenly veers left at what many call the elbow. My eyes realign westward. I stop and look up the incline, which is a perfect straight line to the circle of stones, quarter of a mile distant and fronted by the tall Heel Stone. The line is now picked out by two small paths, little more than sheep trods. Each follows the once glaring chalk bank on either side of the avenue that was perhaps last excavated by Kablea. The right edge of the avenue is silhouetted by the half light whereas in the brightness of summer it could hardly be seen. I move across to the left side of the avenue, equally defined by the low light. Some believe that this orientation, which overlays a series of parallel chalk ridges below the turf, is the reason why Stonehenge was built here. The ridges point east and directly at the summer solstice sunrise. Experts suggest that although the Ice Age glaciers did not reach Wiltshire the cold climate would have exposed the chalk. To ancient people it was a sign from the Gods. For me, the two parallel sides of the avenue take my eye directly to the circle of stones. It should be a moment of heightened spirituality but my senses conspire to spite my cerebral high. Visually, the stone circle is cluttered by three security staff, prominent in high-vis vests, their vehicles parked close by. Further to my right was the transport for the pagans, no longer chariots but motley vans, buses and motorhomes, parked in line along a green road. They formed a colourful scar across the land and over the horizon. Audibly, from my left, a thousand cars an hour send tyre and engine noise across the void from the A303. It is an irony that the great Temple to the sun is gutted by what they now call the highway to the sun. The spoiling intrusion is total; welcome to Stonehenge 2015.

A drone sits on the grass, its flippant technology mocking the stolid stones. Its handset pilot leans against the ugly fence, which prevents entry to the stones. His body is strewn with expensive camera equipment. The security staff harass him; stay out of the restricted area and no flying over the stones. I am prevented from finding a position that will give me a photo of the sunrise behind the stones, my purpose for being here. I have a feeling of panic as I rush down onto the green road. I scurry past the vehicles sheltering druids in white robes, misplaced in representing a period 2000 years after Stonehenge was built. They were resplendent at yesterday's winter solstice, a day cloudy and dull to frustrate photographers like me. I pass by a double-decker bus morphed into a motorhome and scurry about, ending up on the top of a disc barrow, apologising to the dead occupant for my lack of respect. I am standing on the top of what looks like a flying saucer made of turf, the surrounding ditch forming a perfect circle around my craft. I admire the construction yet remind myself that Stonehenge was ancient when these Bronze Age tombs were constructed. Was the site also sacred to them and did they venerate the very view that I seek? The motorised clutter now spoils all but telephoto shots. The sun is higher and I get my shots; the flaming ball over the circle of stones. Technology cheats, as the long lens flies over the bus and something of the prehistoric past is recreated; the eyes and ears are knowing and are not deceived.

A few days later, as I write about Zuri's trip to Stonehenge, the internet features Trip Advisor's 11 worst tourist rip-offs in the UK. Prominent is Stonehenge and one of their reviewer's calls it "a pile of bricks in a field" and states "I despair the abysmal nature of the monument." What influenced this reviewer was the poor presentation of Stonehenge and yet this person appears to lack the ability to interpret the scale and heritage of the monument.

These observations make me wonder how Zuri saw Stonehenge. Apart from her move down the river, Zuri's journey to Stonehenge is her trip of a lifetime. It is not a sabbatical, nor is it to broaden her horizons in any way. It is a true pilgrimage. Stonehenge is her Mecca and all tribal members must at some point in their life visit the Temple. As with the journey to Mecca, the Hajj, it must be a submission and a ritual journey that in itself complements the spiritual awareness that will arise from the experience. It is a supernatural journey, with processions, ritual walking, ceremonies and feasts. The Temple is the focus of their cosmos, the way in which they have ordered the sun, moon and planets. They had to do this without our science and knowledge. The sunfall ceremony is part of the order and there may be many others over the year, some perhaps related to the phases of the moon.

Unlike the San People, who built nothing of substance, Zuri's people have the linear awareness of how the building of Stonehenge had evolved through various stages. Prior to this they had constructed the wood circles and the even older, chambered tombs. They probably knew the purpose of the greater and lesser cursus, the elongated ditched enclosures adjacent to Stonehenge and built a millennia earlier, whose meaning is lost to us now. Whatever, they know they have a past even though nothing is written down. Contrast this to recent findings in the Amazon rainforest which show that tribes there are only aware of living memory and have no sense of their history. Our archaeology reinforces the fact that Stonehenge itself went through many phases over thousands of years. Early farmers created a grassy henge on an already sacred site. They became aware of a bluestone with special powers in the area we now call Prescelli, in Pembrokeshire. So, each autumn, they would send a work party to Prescelli, 140 miles west of Salisbury Plain. They would select perhaps four stones, each weighing up to four tonnes. These would have been hauled to the coast, put onto rafts, floated around Lands End, along the coast and up the sacred River Avon. Did people stand on the banks to greet their arrival? They were farmers and sea people, masters of water. The precise spot where they left the river, to haul the bluestones to Stonehenge, is unknown. Was it along the route that was to become the avenue, the ritual walkway to the circle? This appears to have been formally constructed with banks and ditches hundreds of years later, when the sarsens were erected, yet it may already have existed as a path. This route has an easy gradient from the river but does not go direct to the circle, taking a line up to the highest point and then approaching the circle from the east, on the path of the rising sun. This may have developed because evidence suggests that the site was sacred thousands of years earlier, when it was even more remote. A marked route was then essential, otherwise paths become overgrown as there were so few people. Logic suggests that seekers would follow the river to a set point and follow markers, perhaps cut into trees, to the site. As ritual was fundamental to their psyche it suggests that they would have dragged the bluestones on this route, the route of the forefathers. The present avenue would then overlay this original path.

Ultimately, 56 bluestones were set inside the henge circle and about 80 were used in total. If they brought in four stones each year, it would have taken 20 years. The cremated remains of around 80 men, women and children lined the soil socket beneath these stones. When the bones were dated, they spanned a period of around 250 years. This meant that they either brought in a new stone, or lifted an existing stone as and when somebody died, or retained the remains over this period and then carried out the burials in one later operation. The Gods appreciated their effort because the tribe prospered and this would have been attributed to the bluestones.

Over hundreds of years farming grew in importance. The seasons dominated their thinking and with this there appears increasing ritual regarding the movement of the sun, and perhaps the moon. The bluestone circle was reconfigured a number of times, perhaps integrated with erect wood posts with lintels, creating timber portals that framed or otherwise aligned to the sun or moon. These posts would have rotted away and perhaps a decision was taken to recreate the timber features in stone. As for the source of the stone, we have a mass of dispute. Some say that the sandstone blocks, called sarsen, lay all over Salisbury Plain and were readily hauled to Stonehenge. Others claim that the sarsen was hauled from distant Marlborough Downs, where much still remains on the surface of fields. The precedent was that this stone was used to build nearby Avebury, a huge circle with extensive avenues or lines of sarsens blocks. Let's not get too hung up on this issue but suffice to say that where stone exists locally, it is readily exploited and soon appears in the building of houses and walls. That happened at Marlborough, near Avebury, where sarsen is seen everywhere. That never happened in the Stonehenge area and suggests that no stone existed in that locality. What happened next at Stonehenge was unprecedented. They decided to shape the sarsens; a laborious process using handheld hammer stones made of a harder stone. After this shaping, called dressing, they erected the sarsens to create a circle of uprights topped with a circle of lintels. They used inherent carpenter's skills such as mortise and tenon joints to secure the lintels on the uprights. This circle would be superior and render all other circles as inferior. That decision conflicts with the way the sarsens were erected at Avebury. None of them were dressed and they were seemingly chosen because their natural shapes had a meaning lost to us now. Why would artificially shaped stones, or a linked circle, have more significance? Perhaps they envisioned the ring of coping stones as more able to corral the spirit within the centre. They also ceased the practice of placing cremated remains under stones. None were placed under the sarsens or under the new positions chosen for the bluestones.

The reconfiguration of Stonehenge with sarsens was a far greater enterprise than the earlier bluestone circle. At around the same period they built the largest henge in Britain at what we now call Durrington Walls. At least one archaeologist considers this as the work camp for Stonehenge. It appears to have been used over 40 years and to have been occupied by up to 4000 people. Occupation was for a few months each year, probably leading up to the winter solstice, their sunfall. Over the 40 years, we can assume that each year teams walked to Marlborough Downs, about 48 kilometres distant and located two sarsens. These had to be dug up as exposed stone has a case hardened surface and cannot be easily shaped. They probably hammered off the projecting parts or even crudely shaped them before sliding them onto a wood raft, which was then hauled to Stonehenge. The raft was probably drawn over a series of wood rollers. These would be picked up from behind as the raft rolled forward and carried to the front, keeping the raft and stone inexorably moving onwards. Research has shown that using a raft and rollers halves the number of people needed had the stone been hauled without them. I imagine that only men will form the teams as fit strong women, who could readily participate, will be culturally programmed towards childbearing and protected against heavy injurious labour. Whatever, their mortal frames must have experienced profound exhaustion, serious crushing injuries and perhaps fatalities as they gratified the deities. This massive effort was only possible because of their food surplus and because violence, raiding and the vanity of a warrior society was not a distraction.

As with the bluestones, at least 80 sarsens were hauled, with the heaviest weighing up to 50 tonnes. The halfway point, in what is now considered to have been a 12 day haul, could have been Marden Henge and was perhaps the changing point for fresh teams. Current archaeology suggests that Marden Henge may have been a very significant location. Beyond Marden they had the massive haul up the slope and onto Salisbury Plain, then across to Stonehenge. With the sarsen flat, the visible surfaces were dressed, that is hammered into shape. The underside was dressed at least to head height after the stone was erected.

The mass of stone chips from the dressing has been located immediately north of Stonehenge. The dressing would have exposed the raw, almost white stone.

Before they erected the circle of uprights and lintels they built the trilithons in the centre. These comprise of five pairs of sarsens with a lintel linking each pair. They are the biggest stones and formed a horseshoe shape. The outer circle comprised of 30 uprights linked by 30 lintels, and 75 worked stones were erected in total. The older bluestones were reconfigured within the sarsens. This suggests that there was a master plan and somebody in charge, a mastermind, or does it? Perhaps they put up the trilithons which amazed onlookers and then their vanity took charge. The stones proved impressive and so they continued. With the growing national importance of the site and increasing numbers of people they would then need to enhance the avenue down to the sacred river.

Durrington Walls, the work camp, was a massive henge. Inside, two timber circles were constructed, one of which might have been a pattern for Stonehenge as it appears similar in size. Excavation now proves that where the River Avon abutted Durrington Walls, an avenue ran from the camp down to the river. The avenue was 30 metres wide with banks and standing stones down each side. It had a central walkway 15 metres wide covered in packed flint. The river was wider and deeper than it is now and embarking from this ritual space on a boat, a two mile drift downstream would have taken them to a small bluestone circle on the right bank; the ceremonial entrance of the avenue to Stonehenge. Alongside this section of the river, pits have been excavated full of charcoal, hundreds of worked flints, cattle and pig bones and the scapula of a brown bear. Two pits contained a single scallop shell.

Whilst living at Durrington Walls for a period each autumn the people organized ceremonial feasts using large Grooved Ware pots. Some of these pots could hold 100 litres and suggests communal catering skills. The feasts appear to have been around the winter solstice. Their waste was thrown into a midden. When excavated these contained a mass of animal bones and pottery including Grooved Ware. It appears that not all the meat was eaten, the remainder being thrown into the midden, probably as part of a ritual. The fact that meat and fat could be wasted, that it was an excess, might have been a means of expressing status; that those who created an icon like Stonehenge would prosper. Analysis of the cattle teeth from the midden showed that they were probably reared in Wales and the South West and had been herded to Stonehenge.

Why create Stonehenge? Perhaps, as the winter solstice draws near they had developed a ritual to arrest the descent of the sun. Otherwise, if it continued to fall each day it would lead to perpetual darkness. They also had to ensure that everybody who is to attend is there and at the right time. We can assume that only at Stonehenge can the shamans forecast the date so perhaps they sent a messenger downriver to remind the local shamans when the time was imminent. Those down at Christchurch would need at least three days to paddle or walk to Durrington Walls. How were those in Wales and the South West notified? When all these local shamans came together at the work camp, did they elect a principal shaman to manage all ritual at Stonehenge, similar to an archbishop today? Everything points to somebody being in charge, having the vision to create Stonehenge and to reconfigure and maintain it over many centuries. The social organisation is considerable as many people have to remain on the home ground, including the aged, the ill, the pregnant and those caring for children and farm stock. Neither can they arrange their own sunfall ceremony if their shaman has travelled to Stonehenge. These people also needed to be fed so there must have been a limit on those selected to go to Stonehenge.

Stonehenge is the greatest Neolithic construction and no other henge or stone circle was built after it. Silbury Hill, which was built later, is not a henge or circle and had another purpose. Stonehenge is also the only circle that has proven solar and celestial alignments and it remained in use or was at least protected until after the Romans invaded. It is easy to imagine that people lost confidence in stone and realized, finally, that the henges and circles did not possess the power anticipated of them.

Was it the introduction of metal or perhaps the appearance of the Beaker People that led to the downfall of Stonehenge? In Zuri's time, these people either invaded or drifted from Europe into many parts of the country. They clearly had an impact. Their knowledge of metalworking arrived with new belief patterns, which included individual burial, with grave goods and the Beaker pots. This was the transitional period from the Neolithic Stone Age to the Bronze Age. The first stage of the Bronze Age is sometimes referred to as the Copper Age. With such acquisitions, an elite or warrior class seems to have arisen and perhaps the influence of shamans declined. Axes, many of them ceremonial, in copper and then bronze became the symbols of power. Gold appeared and all this wealth was fuelled by the continuing growth of farming. In another 1000 years the metal tipped plough of the Iron Age will open up the rich clay English soils and the farming power will move west and then to the Midlands, the Thames Valley and the East coast. Avonlands and the Avon, a mere sliver of water meadows betwixt barren chalk downs, is left to slip into decline, reinvigorated to some degree by Medieval sheep farming and the more recent reliance upon oil based fertilizers.

The ceremony, which I call sunfall, is the winter solstice and may have been celebrated from when the glaciers retreated. We have no idea whether it continued to be celebrated at Stonehenge from the Bronze Age, but it appears to have remained a British and European ritual. The Christianised Romans, conscious of their failure at getting people to abandon their pagan rituals, formally placed Christmas into the gap between Saturnalia, the 7 December, and the New Year. Christmas superimposed itself over the pagan ceremony.

We now realize that the site of Stonehenge was sacred much earlier than was originally thought. The town of Amesbury, intimately associated with Stonehenge, is now credited as the longest continuous settlement in the UK, dating from 8820 BC. This has a political dimension because in recent years Neil Oliver, the Scottish historian, has been intent on elevating the Ness of Brodgar in the Orkney Islands as Britain's ancient capital. His claim arose after I began writing this book elevating Avonlands to a similar lofty status. The Ness is a wondrous site and I hesitate to refute his argument but he misses the point. Avonlands, including Amesbury, had the river, the farming, the timber and the equitable climate; all the advantages lacked by remote Scottish islands. The Ness, on the other hand, was abandoned in prehistory and given back to whinberry and heather. Even the Romans retreated from Scotland back to Hadrian's Wall, because they only wanted the grain basket of England. Avonlands and Stonehenge, you see, is Britain's ancient capital.

Chapter 21

Temple of the Sun

A hand pushed her shoulder and Zuri awoke. It was crow black in the hut, but noises could be heard from out in the camp. She put on her skins, conscious that it was cold. She picked up her baby and tucked him inside next to her breast before going outside. Few spoke, the excitement intense but food was their first call. They clustered around the large pot over the fire and using her wood bowl, she scooped out some orzotto, pig meat and grains, but it lacked the soft green leaves of herbs. She missed the green leaves and flowers at this dark time of the year but was too excited to dwell on food and ate silently. Afterwards, she pulled up grass tufts and wiped out her bowl. Kablea pointed her gaze towards the sky, to the seven stars, the cluster that told them how the season was progressing. The stars were so prominent up here on the heights. Kablea had always told her that when the seven stars dropped over the edge of the world, beyond sight, then it was the time to plant seed. The moon glimmered behind light clouds and Zuri felt calm, the moon was always her companion; the glow of the dark. The noisy ring of the camp and its fires, nestled below silent, shadowed hills. Out on the hills the land was unpeopled.

The shaman and shamaness led their group down through the camp and across two open clearings where the wood circles had once stood. She then felt the flint beneath her bare feet and knew that it was the approach to the river. In the dull light they passed between the stone portals and climbed into logboats. Drumming could be heard as it drifted on the wind from where the sun set. They pushed off and floated down on the current, the river twisting and turning this way and that. In one wide loop the moon suddenly flashed up, reflected in the still black water. With no horizons she was disorientated but the shaman reminded them that the bad spirits would also be confused by the twists and turns and could not follow them. When the owls called from the trees as they passed, the shaman called back to them. Everybody sat silent and still as the flow of the water moved the boat, the paddlers unneeded. A fire, reflected in the trees across the river, drew them to the riverbank in a wooded valley. The paddlers had to work hard to turn the boat back against the current and into the bank. They stepped out of the logboat and onto a wood platform, and walked across a narrow causeway. Zuri realized that she was standing in the henge at the start of the avenue. It was where their procession would begin and she could sense from the trodden grass that many other groups had already passed through. The avenue marked the safe passage, the white chalk banks repelling the bad spirits that might take hold of them. They filled their water skins from a spring as there was no water beyond that point. Then they walked and climbed along the avenue, the white banks reflecting the glow of the moon. Slowly, they breasted the hill and turned west and the drumming became louder, floating on the wind into their faces. They crossed an open ridge, a fire burning in the distance, yet little could be seen but the white banks flowing away into the darkness. The ground dropped away so that they could no longer see the fire, and the drumming dulled. The breeze was now on Zuri's right cheek and she knew that they had changed direction. They climbed again to a point where everyone stopped in awe. The white banks, like arrow shafts, took the eye straight to the circle of stones. Beyond the circle, a fire blazed and the light shone through the stones, picking out the shadowy forms of people progressing up the avenue. Zuri had seen nothing like it before and could not speak. As they approached, the stones grew in size and the light from the fire highlighted circles within circles. The rhythmic beat of the drums echoed off the stones.

It was then, from the front of the procession, very softly at first, people began to chant to the rhythm of the drums. The sound grew as each group took up the chant. When they had all passed the great Heel Stone and crossed into the henge, they were all chanting as one. The sound, the sight, filled Zuri's head until it spun and tears ran down her face. The sparks from the fire shot into the darkness and the circle of stones united the earth, the sky and the underworld.

The light crept in like a stealthy wolf but no sun appeared. They knew that they could not enter the stones and continued their way around the outside of the circle. Zuri looked through the sarsens topped with their lintels and over the first circle of bluestones. The huge trilithons, forming an arc, dominated the centre but she could not make out the healing bluestones which stood within them. As the sun peeped above the misty hills the chanting and drumming ceased and the invocation to the light began. Zuri had been told that the shamans would draw the first light into the gape of the trilithons and hold it there, until its release at the sunfall, when it would sink into the underworld.

Later, Zuri gathered with those in need of the healing bluestones. Some, like her, coughed and had a strange pallor, others were on litters and somewhere amongst them was the sick archer. She could not see him as he was surrounded by those who carried his litter and by the many whose curiosity demanded that they view this strange man. The archer was one of the Beaker People, newcomers and yet, for their small numbers they dominated all the talk. They were not farmers and yet prospered. That puzzled Zuri because only farmers flourished in the valley. Although the Beaker People spoke their language, it was different and with so many words that they could not understand. It was Kablea who first told her about these people who traded up and down the river.

The high shamaness then led the healing ceremony. As she moved around the bluestones she beseeched them to drive out the black spirits that caused the ills; that they should return to the underworld. Later, after the high sun, the shamaness called upon the new bearers to approach the stones. Zuri, with her child, waited and in turn had to step forward into the circle and give thanks to the Gods for fertility and the gift of life.

The sun fell and touched the hills and it grew colder as all cloud flew away. Rhythmic drumming called them to the sunfall ceremony where the shamans formed a line and walked towards the circle, the high shaman leading. With a mace in one hand, and a carved staff in the other, he walked beneath the lintels and stood where the light had been embraced by the great trilithons. The drumming stopped and the high shaman called upon the stones to summon down the overworld, to draw up the underworld and unite them within the circle. He asked the Gods to invoke the ancestors to stand beside them to call upon the birds that fly, the animals that walk, to gather within the arms of the Great Bear, that there be harmony and fertility for all things. He asked that the waning sun be filled with strength so that it waned no more, for it to flourish sun by sun, warming the overworld and the underworld and at its zenith to become the spirit of the harvest and the giver of life to all.

Zuri listened and watched the sun sink into the underworld.

Chapter 22

The Advent of Bling

When I first met him he was almost "a skeleton in the cupboard." The proud Amesbury Archer was tucked shabbily into a worn cabinet in the corner of a small, dark and depressing room. As a mourner, perhaps even a distant relative, I was upset and I swore about how pathetic the British are, shamefully hiding this iconic skeleton, this demigod, in a dull corner. I reflected upon how the Europeans acted with so much more pizzazz. When they found Otzi the iceman in the Alps, they presented him as if in state, in the South Tyrol Museum of Archaeology. He is embraced, venerated, almost treated like royalty with no expense spared on research and the way he was presented. Okay, perhaps they exploited him, a marketeer's dream of thousands of tourists, yet they honoured the man. I recall decades ago when on holiday in Italy, one of the tours on offer was an 80 mile coach trip to Bolzano to see Otzi the iceman. But he is no more significant than our Amesbury Archer, a shining star in the world of British archaeology. Since my first visit to Salisbury & South Wiltshire Museum they have moved his skeleton, in effect, his entire grave into The Wessex Gallery, a much improved and exciting space. Unfortunately, the British fudge is to leave such things to cash strapped councils and under resourced museums reliant upon volunteers and public donations. Heritage and culture are near the bottom of the political manifesto, just above the environment and libraries. As for tourism, we entirely miss the marketing trick.

The grave of the Amesbury Archer was found in May 2002 during the building of a new school at Amesbury. He was one of the Beaker People, from what is now Europe, and although they probably never invaded as such, their small numbers had an inverse impact on native culture. Undoubtedly cool, the Beaker men may well have taken their pick of the Avonlands women and the latest research suggests their genes will come to dominate the farmer genes that built Stonehenge. They introduced a new death practice, interring the whole body in an individual grave. They also placed one or more Beakers, their pottery drinking mugs, in the grave and sometimes further possessions. We do not know what Zuri's tribe called these people but due to their influence they must have been the celebs of the day. The archer's grave was one of the first Beaker graves excavated in Britain and was dated to around 2400 – 2200 BC. This latter date is the one I chose for Zuri's story. The archer was around 173 centimetres tall and his body was surrounded by over 100 artefacts including two gold items and three copper knives. The gold and copper was the first ever found in Britain and significantly, this appears to have been his trade. He also wore or had about his body, stone and flint items of superior design and quality to that produced by the local people. Two of these were stone wristguards and one of these appears to have been tied to his wrist with leather straps. Was he drawn to Avonlands because it had a farming surplus and people with products to barter for his rare skills? The copper in his grave appears to have been mined in Spain and the knives forged in that region. These knives introduced the Bronze Age into Stone Age Avonlands. In its earliest years it was more properly called the Copper Age. Although we know copper to be a soft metal, research with copper axes has proved them to be far more efficient than flint. Although the axe edge is soon blunted it can readily be hammered back to sharpness. What Zuri's people did not understand was how metal was going to transform their society. The greatest impact will be millennia later when the iron tipped plough will tame heavy soils. Metal will also have an impact on the Neolithic economy as trade in antler and flint falls away. The farmers appear to have adapted but it sounded the death knell for the diminishing hunter-gatherers in this land.

Ironically, the archer's DNA analysis indicated that he grew up near the Alps, a relative perhaps of Otzi and there are other similarities. The archer was interred with 18 flint arrows whilst Otzi possessed 14 flint arrows. The mixed viburnum and dogwood shafts of Otzi's arrows survived whereas those of the archer had decayed. The archer was aged between 35 and 45 years and Otzi around 45 years when they died. The enigma is that the archer's three knives were of a thin copper and could not have been used for anything substantial, least of all as weapons. One strike on a body and the blade would have snapped. Yet, in a world without markets it occurs to me that this man was a mobile shop front displaying his wares to the affluent farmer of the day. His promotional message was to replace old technology with new. Imagine him, dressed to impress, literally, with gold hair clasps, a luxuriant roeskin over his shoulders, a bow and a quiver of arrows tipped with the finest barbed and tanged flint arrowheads, thin polished stone wristguards and a Kimmeridge shale belt-ring on a richly tooled leather belt. The man, the warrior, is all chutzpah, a strutting peacock, not a bird they knew. He was a flash set in a theatre of bucolic blandness, the other actors all dull farmers with boring scripts about cattle and pigs. He would draw, with some flourish, a tooled leather sheath from his belt, the first ever seen on the river. He would flip open the top and pull out a gleaming copper knife. It would have a shaped wooden handle, embossed with copper nails. Again, nothing like it having been seen before. The thin knife in his grave is either just for show or for ceremony or a sample which he can manufacture in a heavier version for other uses. The buyer barters for it using grain and the archer barters some of the grain for copper ore from the mines in North Wales. He might also barter for cowhide, because his tools suggest that he is a leather worker, this skill displayed in his knife sheath and belt. The man is a specialist, skilled beyond all others bar his kinfolk, a possessor of the secret of metal.

The questions that archaeologists pose in this situation include, why does the archer have these artefacts in the grave and why is he buried in this way? The obvious response is that these items equipped the archer with all he needed to survive in the next world. This man possesses an ego beyond all deference to Zuri's tribal belief and communalism. We can reliably accept that he did not complete a will or funeral directive before he died but his kin knew what kind of burial he would have wanted and made it happen in a potentially hostile environment. His belief, much like the distant Egyptians, was of individualism, of a rebirth into a world where he would pick up his old trade and so needed his tools and theatre set to survive. This culture or similar would inter a warrior in my street perhaps 500 years later. The old Gods, unity between all living things, are dead.

The next question is what killed the archer? His skeleton displays an eroded hole in his lower jawbone which would have been pus filled, extremely painful and odorous. In these cases death can occur from septicaemia or from swelling blocking the airway. His teeth look good, as do the teeth of so many skeletons from his period. Why are tooth abscesses so frequent in skeletons and often cited, as with the archer, as a potential cause of death? A tooth abscess, I assumed, typically arises from a mouth full of neglected teeth and a diet full of sugar, neither of which could apply to the archer. As he must have travelled by sea and river, he will have eaten lots of fish, perhaps dried fish, albeit for short periods. Fish bones can easily puncture and infect the gums, causing an abscess. Dried fish is lightweight and yet nutritious when hydrated in fresh water but attracts flies whilst in the drying and storage over long periods. The flies can infect food by walking, vomiting and defecating on it. Was it an infected fish bone that felled the archer? The evidence points otherwise. Recent research suggests that the Beaker People ate only meat and dairy and drank blood or beer or a similar alcoholic beverage.

Neither do their teeth show signs of scratches that imply bread eating. It is the grinding of the flour using querns that puts grit into the bread, which then wears down the teeth.

I have already partly answered another of the questions pitched at the archer. Why was he at Stonehenge? More especially, why was he at a Stonehenge that seemingly had no significance to him or his culture. Assuming that he was not there just to trade then some archaeologists suggest that his failing health was the reason. Was Stonehenge the Lourdes of the day? Was it known as a healing centre right into Europe? Other than his jaw abscess his left kneecap was missing and the joint potentially inflamed due to infection. He would have walked with a pronounced limp. Analysis indicates that he lived only a short time in England but had also spent a limited time in Wales. Copper ore exists in Wales on Great Orme's Head, so was he involved in the exploitation of the ore? The Great Orme towers over the sea and is adjacent to a safe harbour on the River Conwy, part of the coastal trading routes. The ore would have been too heavy to carry overland and will have been transported by boat.

The archer's alchemy was that of turning stone into a hard adaptable substance, which was revolutionary and must have appeared supernatural. Would Zuri and her people have feared him because of his impact on her culture? It is not dissimilar to the way the gerontocracy fears the impact of immigrants and the internet on our culture.

The archer is our first example of individual male status and he might justifiably be called a warrior. Little evidence of status existed. One example is the way the farmers considered the hunter-gatherers as socially and technologically inferior. The farmers were removing trees and taking over riverside land, constantly pushing back the wildlife upon which the hunter-gatherers relied. Yet the evidence shows that farmers still hunted, either to supplement their diet or because hunting is deeply ingrained. The hunt persists today in the continuing support for fox hunting, especially in the gerontocracy. The heavily armed archer is perhaps the first evidence of what we now call marketing. He provided the model for a return of a more sophisticated hunter, rebranded for a changing society. The hunter is no longer the flea-bitten hunter-gatherer on the margins of survival but is equipped with a new image in order to snare a new quarry, the wealthy farmer.

The archer is also thought to have ridden a horse. If true, he would have been astride an animal similar to an Exmoor or New Forest pony and not some great charger. The existence of ponies in Britain is not resolved. Some believe that the Exmoor pony survived the Ice Age and remained here but many dispute this. Riding would also have been tortuous with no bridleways and with overhanging trees and bushes constantly trying to unseat a rider. No cross country routes have been identified from that time although riding alongside rivers and the coast may have been feasible. Research suggests that humans first rode horses in Spain in 3000 BC. If true, then horses and riding could have spread overland through Europe and thus reached Britain much later; or did it move along the coast and arrive here before the rest of Europe?

As for Zuri, did she feel envy towards the archer? He was the first exponent of bling in these islands and of the corrupting power of stuff, in this case copper and gold. The man is flashy, conspicuous and pretentious, outshines the shamans and challenges the Gods. The have's are pitched against the have not's. This archer man and his kinfolk will destroy the communal life that had lasted perhaps 8000 years. The shared ownership and absence of envy would be lost, replaced eventually by Rolex, Apple and Lamborghini.

Does Zuri realize that the archer epitomises men in the ascendancy? If so, then she would have to recognize that she was equal to men and therefore subject to being demeaned. It is evident to us now that the Bronze Age spawned an elite, perhaps a male warrior culture, who gathered possessions and with them, power. The brown skinned rustic like Zuri immediately loses all grace to the woman who wears stuff, has pale skin because she does not toil in the water meadows or smell of sweat. The woman herself becomes a possession, a thing of desire rather than another hand in the harvest. The few Beaker graves excavated contain weapons with men and shale or jet beads with women; the sexes are clearly delineated for the first time. We can anticipate Zuri, at some stage, worrying about the affect of wild weather on her skin and was she ever heard to say "Does my bum look big in this deerskin?"

It is the graves of men, not women, in which we find the Beakers and some of these show traces of an alcoholic drink. Also, their graves contain the tang and barb arrowheads. These are a sophisticated design that pierces the flesh and remains embedded where other arrowheads would potentially fall out. The arrowheads are so thin that they lack the robustness necessary for actual use. Some suggest that all these grave objects were given as gifts by mourners. If that were true then surely many less exceptional items would have been given by those with lesser skills and resources, such as bone necklaces but these are not apparent. I am not aware of any culture where grave goods are sorted and the inferior ones rejected. It also appears that Beaker graves were not filled in immediately. This was surmised after the skeleton of a frog was found in a Beaker grave near Avebury and it was assumed to have crept in before the backfilling.

Because the archer's bling came out of stone, Zuri and her people lost confidence in the sarsens. They are not aware that Stonehenge will fall into a steady decline, an icon to the achievements of the forefathers but no longer relevant to the changing deities. The secular gerontocracy treat our cathedrals in much the same way; a desire to conserve them only because they speak of past endeavours. Religious fervour is now to be feared.

Chapter 23

The Ill Wind

Zuri was told that the breath had gone out of the archer. She knew that they would delay their return to the homeland because they had been called upon to bear witness to his burial. These strange people with their metal and pots and new ways had swept in like a great storm. The shamaness was untroubled and in no doubt that these things would pass. Her steadfastness was her very weakness because when asked where these people had come from and why they had the gift of metal, she could not say. Even she had accepted that nobody could remember such a thing in the past; that change had always happened through the tribe, through talking and working together. Never had a man stood out like this, a wolf that gnawed at the way they lived.

Zuri found that there was little food for her to forage, it was cold and her cough shook her body. Up here on the white rock the grass was thin and not lush as in the water meadows. This was the grass of her childhood, where people could not grow grain. All talk was about the archer and Kablea had told her that he would not enter the underworld as they did. His whole body would be put into the ground and the white rock placed over him. They could not understand how his spirit could be freed from the body. It would be trapped and could not move between the overworld and underworld.

The archer's burial was to be at the next sun and his kinfolk had chosen the place close to where they had their huts. This was away from the work camp, on the high ground looking down to the river and across to the great circle on the horizon, where the sun set. Zuri and Kablea, all of them, would beach a short way downriver and walk to where he was to be laid out.

They beached the boat, then followed the path up the hill

and joined a mass of people where the ground levelled out. The archer's body was on a wood platform so that people could walk by and see all that he was. Dressed in skins, he was placed on his left side, with his knees slightly bent, as if asleep. His kinfolk stood about, ushering people, watching, whilst others dug with antler picks into the white rock. Much as she feared him Zuri was intent on moving as close to him as she could; to see but not to touch. People slowly moved forward, looking and whispering. Suddenly, she was staring into his bearded face outlined by his jet black hair. It was braided with two clasps made of gold, shining like small suns. They had a smooth lustrous colour and were thin like the finest shell, each with a line of decorative dots along the edge. What did the gold mean? Was it just adornment or an amulet, something that gave him protection?

Kablea had told her that the archer had travelled to their valley from beyond the sea, where ice and snow lay so high that it linked the earth to the sky. Had he flown to them, as the shaman had said that he could fly to other worlds? But the shaman had never told them of this new substance, this metal, which came out of stone. The stone in the shaman's mace and the jadeite axe had been their contact with the Gods and yet it had never given them this metal. Kablea's forefathers had dragged bluestones from the land of the setting sun and also hammered the great sarsens into shapes. Why had the Gods kept this secret from them? Had the stones given up their power? Why were the archer's kin the only ones who knew the secret? They could remove the power of the stone using fire, like taking marrow from a bone. Yet, the metal still had to be crafted; shaped, decorated and polished until it shone.

It was the archer's knives that Kablea's eyes were drawn to. Three had been removed from their crafted leather pouches and placed beside his body. The knives lay glistening and sharp pointed. They were made for cutting up the body of an animal or cutting away skin. Now, for Kablea, flint tools would never be the same; they were diminished. He called the metal cobrea and had told Zuri that the knives were sharp, even sharper than the black flint. He did not say that they could be used for stabbing people but others talked of this. They would, Zuri thought, be given to one of his kinsman so that the power would go from one man to another.

Beside the archer's body was his cushion stone, small enough to fit into the palm of his hand. People said that this also had great power. He would hammer his metal over and around different parts of the cushion stone to create shapes. This was his crafting skill. Some of his possessions were not unknown to Zuri. There were four boar's teeth and people said that he used them to make the cobrea glow. Zuri's talisman was a tooth from the lusty boar that defended the Gods and it upset her that he was able to use them in this way.

The archer had an empty quiver as the arrows had been removed and strewn around his body by his kinfolk. They said that he must not let loose any arrows; that they had to be kept apart from the bow, which was at his shoulder. This was to show the Gods that he would not take up his weapons whilst on his journey but would need them in his new world. Some men talked otherwise, that although he looked disarmed, it was a feint and he could quickly take up his warrior stance. They said that this was because his forearm displayed his leather bracer to protect against the lash of the bowstring. Tied over this was his wristguard made of black mudstone, ground very thin and shaped like a short razor shell. A hole had been ground at each end and Zuri was astounded at how perfect the crafting was. Each hole was even and smooth so that a leather thong could hold it in place. A second wristguard, in red mudstone, lay nearby. Neither wristguard showed any signs of wear from the repeated lash of the bowstring; they were smooth and unmarked. Kablea said that these stone wristguards were adornments and made to be seen.

People moved forward to where they would place the archer in the ground. His kinfolk had picked out the grave and then hammered in wood staves to hold up the sides. The floor, cut into the white rock, appeared bright and smooth. Zuri could imagine him inside, covered by a great mound made from the white rock they had removed.

Kablea said that he was to be laid on his left side, his face looking away from the sun. Zuri suddenly realized that the way his body was presented on the wood platform was the way that they would bury him. That they would lift him up and place him just as he was. She understood at that moment what Kablea had been trying to tell her, that his knives and his gold, all these items laid about would stay with him and not be passed on to his kinfolk. She was disbelieving, that these objects were going to accompany him on his journey.

The body and all the items were placed in the grave. Five Beakers were then brought out, each crafted with strange patterns and containing food and drink that would feed him on his journey. Each Beaker was carefully positioned around his body. The grave was to remain open for some suns and would be guarded by his kinfolk to prevent birds, animals and people, from disturbing the archer and his possessions.

Zuri and the others walked back down the hill, pushed off their logboat and drifted with the current. As the light failed, they beached again to spend the dark on the riverbank beneath their skins. As the light returned the shaman cried out that he had lost his jadeite axe. He was distraught because it had come down to him with all its power through many forefathers. He would be scorned, derided for all time and he trembled. The tether on the axe had snapped and although they had searched and searched they could not find it; it was a bad omen.

They continued down the river in silence. The rain poured down and the river blended with the sky; all was wet. But it was the lashing wind that hurt Zuri most. She felt the cold in her bones and her shoulder skin was sodden and weighed heavily. She coughed and spat, unaware that the spittle was red, like the embers of the fire.

Chapter 24

The Innocent Blue Tit

I inhabit parallel worlds of two tribes separated by a blip of time. It is a linear history, one that has morphed culture into culture, creating a bastard people, a mixture yet essentially European. I accept that the gerontocracy is little more than a small facet of our culture, essentially white and middle class, yet it is the vanguard facing death and any world that follows. Unlike with Zuri and her certainties it is now surrounded by tribulation and age old religions seem to offer little in the way of relief. For many, it is a life too long in the ending, the fear being that gradual loss of consciousness until you have no idea who you are. A battalion of doctors, nurses and carers sit in the wings, all committed to keeping us alive no matter what the quality of life. Unlike with Zuri it is now difficult to die.

For Zuri, the rituals around death and disposing of the dead were dictated by the deities, by belief patterns. Everybody followed the same procedure, which was why the archer's burial was so controversial. For her, it was also a matter of pragmatism, that which could be achieved within the limits of technology, finance and resources. In attempting to analyse what happened in her time, the problem is that the majority of the bodies are missing. No cemeteries have been found to indicate what practices they followed. The archaeology is little help because it tends to focus on artefacts whereas ritual leaves few traces.

What is evident is the physical effort that Zuri and Kablea faced in order to survive. They could not stop farming and foraging to dig a grave with an antler pick every time somebody died. They would need to excavate a deep grave in order to frustrate the efforts of wolves and bears and all the other animals scenting the tasty carrion below ground. Neither is cremation feasible for routine deaths.

The evidence suggests that as farming developed around 3800 BC in places such as Christchurch the people built chambered tombs. The earliest versions were probably made of wood and later of stone. They constructed a passage some metres long, crouching height at the entrance and leading to one, two or three chambers, often just high enough to enable a person to stand. Many see these constructions as emblematic of caves, the passage an access to the underworld. These chambers were covered with soil or gravels which were sometimes layered, probably for ritual reasons. This soil or gravel often extended well beyond the back of the chamber, what is referred to as a tail. No interior painted art work has been found and carvings are extremely rare. Wood figures or idols may have existed but will have since rotted away. Evidence of at least one chamber exists in Christchurch but others may have been destroyed or have sunk into the ground.

Early assumptions by archaeologists were that bodies were placed in the chamber and allowed to decompose. The bones would later be cleaned and retained for rituals, which might have included deposition in rivers. What conflicts with this theory is that too few chambers appear to have existed to accommodate the number of deaths. Secondly, the catacomb, which is effectively what they are, is a practicable process only in hot countries with low rainfall and where bodies dehydrate rapidly. This process does not work in our wet and cool climate. The chambered tombs would have been damp and decomposition would have led to a mass of body fluid coating the floor. As most bodies would have been children with few hard bones, the amount of decomposing tissue would be considerable. Within decades this organic ooze would make entering the tomb hazardous and unpleasant, flies would proliferate, the smell would be nauseating and vermin and other animals would be attracted. None of this would be conducive to holding ceremonies in the vicinity. I believe, as do many, that the tombs were just a place to store bones. Sometime between 4000 – 3000 BC the use of the chambered tombs ceased and they were ritually sealed up.

The archaeologists now suggest that cremation/burial became the new ritual for disposing of bodies. The practice involved cremation followed by burial as an integrated process. I remain sceptical of this being a ritual for the everyday funeral. A cremation pyre demands a massive labour input in cutting and collecting timber, which has more value for building and domestic use. I have no problem accepting cremation for a few elite in that it mirrors the current situation in countries such as Tibet and Mongolia. There, cremation is reserved for high lamas and dignitaries whereas the common people use a less intensive process which we refer to as sky burial.

From the few Neolithic cremated remains found in Britain it appears that the cremation pyres were built using hazel and other small easily cut timber, probably grown as coppice. But Avonlands and the chalk downs were never heavily wooded and trees were rapidly being cut down as the population grew. A Neolithic timber pyre required wood that had been dried for up to two summers. Whether damp or dry, wood fires fall far short of the 1100°C of a modern cremator. The skin and outer surface of the body is easily cremated but the muscle tissue and particularly that of younger male bodies, is difficult to break down. The pyre must be well constructed because if one side burns out then the body can easily topple and be thrown off the fire. Once the charred body is in the embers, oxygen is denied and there is none of the volatility of the gas jet of a modern cremator. Hence, the dense flesh just smoulders over a long period. Today in India, an untouchable sits beside the body for days, feeding fresh kindling under the resilient tissue because so few families can afford the cost of a large pyre. This ancient Hindu and Sikh ritual is carried out in order to free the spirit from the body. Science now proves that the pollution from these pyres is immense. Neither is the smell acceptable to most modern western noses.

Cremation experts are aware that bones are oxidized in a modern cremator which makes them easier to break up. This is not the case with pyre cremations, the bones staying hard and organic and subject to theft by animals. Consequently, a vigil must be held by the fire and when cool enough, the bones removed by hand. Even today many cremation cultures are content to remove only the larger bones and ignore the smaller. Perhaps this was the practice in Avonlands. Archaeologists usually find around one kilo of cremated remains for each body, which is about half of the expected weight arising with a modern cremation. This excludes the use of a wood coffin, which can double the amount of remains.

Neolithic people were also smaller than us and presumably lighter in weight, but this might be compensated for by their bone density. Due to heavy labour, walking and with many running in order to hunt, their bone density and mass would be high. This is the opposite of modern people experiencing an epidemic of osteoporosis and being relatively less active. When ancient cremated remains are found the bones are often broken into small fragments, a ritual probably carried out by select people using ceremonial stone tools. Deposits of cremated remains are occasionally found cut into recesses in chalk graves and were probably contained in a leather bag or birch bark box, which has subsequently rotted away.

Why did they choose cremation for the elite in the Late Neolithic? Some suggest that cremation might have been generated by Sun God worship, which supports the use of fire. Unlike in Egypt, no images to support this have been found. Other experts will suggest that cremation is a means of purifying the dead. If so, the burial of the ashes and effectively de-purifying them in contact with soil makes no sense. There is also a theory that cremation is a sacrificial ceremony, perhaps related to fertility rites, following which the ashes were then scattered. The fact that few bone fragments are found in fields disputes this suggestion. My preference is that the cremation is purely utilitarian, a means of reducing a large body to a small peripatetic pile of remains. This makes them easy to move elsewhere and to be placed in positions not suitable for a full body, such as under the bluestones at Stonehenge. They can also be easily removed and reinterred when a new ritual site is being prepared.

Limited cremation continued up to the introduction of Christianity, when individual burial became routine both for the elite and commoners. From around AD 800 the British were all buried in the local churchyard until urbanisation necessitated the introduction of cemeteries in Victorian times. Cremation as we know it today was also a Victorian innovation and when they were ignorant of how incineration harms the environment. Now when we die, 80% of us choose cremation. The pollutants are filtered out but cannot be recycled and have to be stored. The remaining 20% of deaths utilize burial and since 1993 an increasing number choose natural burial. With over 300 natural burial sites the body will go under a tree, in an orchard or in a wildflower meadow; it is recycled and the burial area becomes an environmental facility, a gift to the community. Zuri would be comfortable with this green and spiritual option, unaware that science now confirms that when buried this way our atoms continue their existence elsewhere in the ecosystem.

Perhaps it is opportune to ask why the gerontocracy favours cremation at the current time. The answer is because it renders a body into sterile and odourless ashes contained in an easily handled casket. The image of decomposition disappears behind a velour curtain. Out of sight, the fat and protein, the nutritious elements in the body are wasted. What is disarming is that nature can be more efficient than a sophisticated cremator. The ancients could not know this and yet their process was efficient, environmental and spiritual. The perceptive reader will see where this is going; sky burial, exposure to birds.

The linear way in which sky burial developed is easy to imagine. The first people, the hunter-gatherers, lived on the margins and had to be pragmatic and so bodies will have been exposed to animals and birds. Over time, they adopted, validated even, this process through myths like that of the Great Bear who, when he dies is eaten by birds. Zuri's people will have used the process because their forefathers used it.

This is not a flight of fancy because I can illustrate nature's incredible alternative. There was an unfortunate incident when a female walker in the Pyrenees plunged over a cliff in 2013. Friends walking with her called the police and they took 50 minutes to visually locate her body from a helicopter. The delay was because the body was obscured by gorging Griffon Vultures. By the time pedestrian rescuers reached the site the birds had stripped her body of all flesh and only a few bones remained. She was fully clothed so that must have slowed the process to some degree. We might assume that this woman, a mountain walker, was fit and well and not on any medication because vultures appear to reject cadavers contaminated with drugs and medicines.

Tibetan sky burial requires that the body be entirely crushed before exposure so that the vultures eat everything. It appears that the Pre-durotriges wanted to retain some bones, so the archaeologists prefer the term excarnation. This is the removal of flesh and organs from the body but leaving most of the bones intact. Unlike animals which have thick hides we have thin skin and it should come as no surprise that so many birds can readily access a sun blushed human thigh. If a naked body is exposed on top of a tower, its height would offer safety for all birds. Large species such as eagles, even heavier when fed, would be able to take flight easily. Locally, equilibrium would be reached between the number of birds and the quantity of bodies being offered.

On the banks of the River Avon just below Woodhenge and Durrington Walls, Mike Parker Pearson's archaeological excavations found three sets of postholes, each with four posts forming a square. They had been surrounded by a palisade, a fence of posts driven into the ground. The largest posts in the squares were 50 centimetres across and estimated at over five metres high. The conclusion was that they were sky towers looking out over the river and presumed to be supporting platforms. This is not such a surprise because there have been suggestions that the earlier causewayed enclosures fulfilled this purpose. These circular ritual spaces, inside a bank and ditch, could have been one of the earliest designs for exposing bodies to birds and animals. They might have progressed to towers as they created more efficient flint axes to cut timber. Also, they may not have wanted animals, particularly with the wolf's apocryphal reputation for liking human flesh, to run off with an entire leg or arm. Even pagans might have seen this as an indelicacy. A sky tower would be a sophisticated solution because it allows only birds to feed on the body. Today, we as a nation have an innate love of birds; we protect and nurture them. Is this embedded in our DNA due to our unique relationship in the past? Even the later Celts believed that birds held our spirits and souls.

Tibet is the one place in the world where sky burial might have persisted from the Stone Age. They consider the vulture a form of angel and they are venerated. Avonlands has a richer and more diverse environment than Tibet. Here, far more species of birds would arrive to feed, including buzzards, kites, ravens, carrion crows, gulls and many smaller birds such as blue tits. Perhaps this is where these little birds developed their liking for fat. In Zuri's time we can add golden eagles and white-tailed sea eagles. The latter would have been the monarch of the sky towers. Its natural habitat was here on our mild coast and not in the Scottish Islands as it is today. It is not a cliff dweller and prefers to nest in trees, ideally pines, which abounded then as now on our heathland. Its nature is to feed on the nearest available food source, usually carrion and the sky towers would be a routine visit for this bird. With humans to consume it would not have to waste energy regurgitating pellets of fur, feathers and hide and can digest small human bones. We are the perfect eagle food and yet sometime later we drove them to extinction. There are also many less conspicuous birds who would feed on us. In 2015 a nature report mentions turnstones, a small wader, feeding on a human body washed up in Anglesey. As for European vultures, more than 100 sightings were recorded over the south of Britain in 2013. Maybe their DNA recalls a time when the British offered them fine dining. Kablea calls them the shuffling birds.

The way that birds utilize carrion appears ill researched but a pattern is usually evident in African wildlife films. The larger birds such as eagles take precedence and prefer muscle tissue and blood rich organs. The vultures follow up and eat anything including intestines and gut. They also swallow small fleshed bones, so those of the feet and hands might be taken. I became intrigued by the Bearded Vulture, a rare European species, which specializes in cracking open marrow rich bones. To obtain the marrow it will carry large bones up into the sky and drop them on a hard surface in order to break them open. Did it actually learn this bone dropping skill from taking the bones offered up in our bodies?

Once the bones had been cleaned off by the birds the skull and other remaining bones could then be deposited in sacred places or hung on or in their huts as memento mori. By then the odour would have disappeared, which from a decomposing human body is like no other. Perhaps sky burial continued for the majority of people and was phased out only after contact with the Romans, who may have used such practices to define paganism. If so, excarnation for the majority and cremation for the elite removes their bones from the archaeological record;

no later DNA analysis is possible. The Beaker people, the only ones to favour burial, leave their bones in the soil and their later sampling for DNA suggests they dominated our society. This must be treated with scepticism as perhaps 90% of the genes of those who built Stonehenge are missing.

Sky burial had never appealed to me and yet after my research I could understand how much it offered to Zuri's people. But, as they prospered and created surplus food they could exalt their elite using the alternative process of cremation. If you think about it, cremation would appear familiar to them. Firstly, the body on a pyre looks like a body on a tower. Secondly, it does what sky burial does, it quickly renders the body to a few bones. Thirdly, it enables them to control the disposal process and avoid the fact that with sky burial, at times of high death rate, the birds will be sated and thereby slower in consuming the bodies. Finally, cremation offers the benefit of drama, of the blazing pyre and for some people the spirit can be seen to exit the body.

As for us nowadays in the UK we are restricted to earth burial or cremation; neither sky burial nor a pyre is legally acceptable.

I think of Zuri and how she is soon to leave her world. It will be a family led funeral with no professional undertakers or embalmers. It will occur soon after death and follow an age old process and ritual. Nothing will be recorded. Death is both common and a routine known to all, and operates parallel to life. Their dead stay with them in spirit and are animated when they see and touch the bones. There is no end with Zuri's death, only the loss of her utility; her skills and mothering. Because of this her kinfolk will not suffer the depression and negativity that surrounds our modern deaths. History would say that she has no memorial but it misleads. You and I have become her living memorial in the unbroken line of genes. Perversely, we dread anonymity after death and so the marketeers sell us the permanence of a bronze plaque or even a granite memorial, the stone now sourced from China. Few realize that research shows that after 15 years less than 10% of mourners return to such memorials and almost nobody after 50 years. In this digital age tangible memorials like this are becoming outdated. Bereaved kin or executors now have to make the onerous decision of whether to maintain a person's online presence after death; remove it or turn it into a digital memorial. We are exterminated by one press of the delete key.

Chapter 25

Feeding the Birds

Kablea stared at Zuri, her eyes open even though the breath had left her body and she had no movement. Was there, in the corner of her mouth, a smile? She had tried to form words as the breath left her and he knew that she had seen the sacred river and the Great Bear. The journey was now to begin and her body must be proffered during the light and before the coming of the dark. First, the shamaness brought the baby to the hut to sever him from his mother's bond. She laid him on Zuri's chest and he clung to her. Then, as Kablea watched, the baby sensed something alien, that the odour was no longer that of his mother; there was no warmth. He began to cry. The shamaness took him up but unable to comfort him, passed him to a bearer. She was one who had an abundance of milk, sufficient for her own baby and for Zuri's. She had fed the baby for many suns as the coughing sickness had dried Zuri's breasts.

Kablea, with others of the family, tied Zuri's thin body to three hazel staves. She was naked except for her boar's tooth talisman. They used nettle cord as, unlike animal gut, it would not be eaten by the birds which would release the body from the staves. They had selected firm, long, hazel staves that would project beyond her head and feet. Some cross pieces held the staves in place. He had seen many bodies proffered and he knew how it must be done, that it was for him to attend to her body, to tie down the limbs and ensure that she would not be dropped. From when he was small he had seen this ritual and as he grew he had always taken part. He laid Zuri so that her stomach and breasts were uppermost and the patriarch brought him the deerskin, the one that their forefathers had always used to cover a body on its last journey. Kablea tied this lightly around Zuri and with his kinsman, they took the stave ends and carried her with ease. The staves lightly flexed as they moved and creaked as bark rubbed bark.

They entered the great circle of Hartz Ahoa from the sunfall side, the overshadow but would walk into the sun as they left. This would reverse Zuri's passage across the circle when she had become an unbearer; one who was to create a life. They laid her down gently in the centre of the henge in front of the great cove. Birds wheeled above and cried out as the men, women and children linked hands and formed a circle around Zuri. The shamaness stood looking over her body and she placed a mark of black on her forehead, the sign of the bearer, so that the Gods would know that she had been favoured with child. She spoke the words of release to ease Zuri's passage to the ancestors. Then, moving on to the entrustment she asked the birds of the light to consume her flesh and release her spirit as they had done for the Great Bear when it made their land.

As her words ended, they lifted Zuri and walked forward until they broke through the circle of people to release her from the tribe. Only the kinfolk could follow on the path of the breathless, which twisted and turned so that her spirit could not find its way back to Hartz Ahoa.

The tower when it was reached was silhouetted against the sea. Birds perched upon it but took flight, circling around, aware that they could soon return. Kablea climbed the tower and with help pulled her litter up and onto the platform. He tied the staves down to make her secure. Finally, he removed and folded the deerskin covering her body. Before climbing down to join his kinfolk he touched the boar's tooth around her neck.

As they slowly moved away the cries of the birds rose in pitch. Some birds settled on the tower edge but most were wheeling about and all were wary. A white tail then swept in casting its shadow over Zuri's body and all the birds scattered, never far, watchful and waiting their turn. The bird stood imperious over her and looked about, silent master of the tower. Then, as if called from above, its hookbeak cut into her body taking the flesh in small pieces until it was sated. It then swept off the edge of the tower with a rush of wind and took flight with ease. The white tails were the biggest of the hookbeaks. They dwelt on the edge of the world, always where the land met the sea. People knew their nests in the tall pine trees along the shore and revered them. They could often be seen wheeling, higher and higher, to become tiny dark specks before disappearing into the overworld.

Watching from the sands, squabbling and noisy, yet cowering to the hookbeaks were the shuffling birds with their crook necks. Before they could move, black birds swooped upon her body taking some of the flesh, now cut and exposed by the hookbeaks. These opportunists gorged and only flew away as the shuffling birds, like a storm of feathers, swept over her body and covered it with lashing rippling wings, each bird lost in the body of another. They ate blindly, fighting over pieces and rending them, often forcing scraps over the edge of the platform, where they dropped onto the ground. Here other birds, those with forked tails, the black birds and the sea birds, swooped around, screeching, occasionally lunging forward if they saw an opportunity. As her body slowly shrank the shuffling birds flew off or stood about, sated. The remaining birds read the signs and moved in. Free of fear, even the smaller birds swelled in number and they all filled the skies; their calls and shrieking grew louder and louder. As the birds slowly decreased in numbers they were replaced by the foragers, the tiny birds, some in twittering flocks hanging off the timbers, even hanging off the bones and seeking out the remaining morsels of fat and skin.

After three suns Kablea walked to the tower to meet those keeping the vigil. They knew the birds and told him that it was the time; he climbed the tower and looked at what remained. He could still make out her hair and the talisman around her neck. The flesh had gone from her bones and it was good. He laid her skeleton on a skin, bound this up and passed it down. At the river he opened the skin and used his flint knife to prise her skull from her neck and put this aside with the long bones. He picked up what remained and together with her talisman, carried them out into the water, releasing them into the flowing current. Back on the shore he used his antler point to scour out what the birds could not reach inside the skull. He then washed the skull and the long bones in the sweet water.

When the next sun rose, the kinfolk gathered outside Zuri's hut for the homecoming. The shamaness held Zuri's skull aloft and welcomed it back as an ancestor. She implored her to watch over them, to keep away ill spirits and to protect them from harm. Her skull was then passed from person to person until it lay in Kablea's hands. He then secured it above the portal inside the hut knowing that Zuri would always be with them.

In the dark, before the rise of the next sun Kablea took Zuri's long bones and placed them in the logboat. He would return them to her family in the wildwood. The patriarch would be with him as head of the family to beseech them to make agreement for another union.

Chapter 26

Postscript

It is only because I live in Christchurch that I have been able to form my relationship with Zuri and our ancestors. It is a relationship that stretches back a mere 4000 years. The gerontocracy and Zuri, both bit players in the evolution of Avonlands.

As I walk above the cliffs, a thrush sings melodiously and the repeated refrain of a chiffchaff reverberates from the tree tops. The waves murmur through the sullen Holm oaks; or is it the sound of the wind sighing through the trees, what the dictionary refers to as soughing? A rabbit crosses my path and it is a prompt to the changes that have occurred since Zuri's time. The bunnies came over with the Normans and Holm oaks were brought in by the Victorians, yet I am heartened that so much remains unchanged; the sun, the sea and the birds, the perpetual trio.

Looking out through the oaks, across the bay to the Isle of Wight, I see the Needles gleam. Within me, Zuri sees the chalk portals of the white island, guardian of the approach to Avonlands. Zuri's world must die, the breath sucked out by the cessation of the narrative. If she is a myth, then perhaps she is more durable even, than granite.

OTHER BOOKS BY THE AUTHOR

A GUIDE TO NATURAL BURIAL
The author, the pioneer of the world's first natural burial site,
explores the myriad social, economic and environmental issues
surrounding the concept of natural burial.
ISBN 978 0 4140 4490 6 Shaw & Sons 276 pages
Published 2010 by Thompson Reuters (Legal) Ltd.

R.I.P. OFF! OR THE BRITISH WAY OF DEATH
An irreverent fictionalized tale of real and astonishing events
beginning in 1993. At times deadly serious; at times, deadly
funny. It's the mysterious world of funeral directors, as they try
to kill off burial under trees and oppose DIY funerals.
ISBN 978 1783061 488 Published by Matador 2013 261 pages

HISTORY

Chronos Books is an historical non-fiction imprint. Chronos publishes real history for real people; bringing to life people, places and events in an imaginative, easy-to-digest and accessible way - histories that pass on their stories to a generation of new readers.
If you have enjoyed this book, why not tell other readers by posting a review on your preferred book site.

Recent bestsellers from Chronos Books are:

Lady Katherine Knollys
The Unacknowledged Daughter of King Henry VIII
Sarah-Beth Watkins
A comprehensive account of Katherine Knollys' questionable
paternity, her previously unexplored life in the Tudor court
and her intriguing relationship with Elizabeth I.
Paperback: 978-1-78279-585-8 ebook: 978-1-78279-584-1

Cromwell was Framed
Ireland 1649
Tom Reilly
Revealed: The definitive research that proves the Irish nation
owes Oliver Cromwell a huge posthumous apology for
wrongly convicting him of civilian atrocities in 1649.
Paperback: 978-1-78279-516-2 ebook: 978-1-78279-515-5

Why The CIA Killed JFK and Malcolm X
The Secret Drug Trade in Laos
John Koerner
A new groundbreaking work presenting evidence that the CIA
silenced JFK to protect its secret drug trade in Laos.
Paperback: 978-1-78279-701-2 ebook: 978-1-78279-700-5

The Disappearing Ninth Legion
A Popular History
Mark Olly
The Disappearing Ninth Legion examines hard evidence for the
foundation, development, mysterious disappearance, or possi-
ble continuation of Rome's lost Legion.
Paperback: 978-1-84694-559-5 ebook: 978-1-84694-931-9

Beaten But Not Defeated
Siegfried Moos - A German anti-Nazi who settled in Britain
Merilyn Moos
Siegi Moos, an anti-Nazi and active member of the German
Communist Party, escaped Germany in 1933 and, exiled in
Britain, sought another route to the transformation
of capitalism.
Paperback: 978-1-78279-677-0 ebook: 978-1-78279-676-3

A Schoolboy's Wartime Letters
An evacuee's life in WWII — A Personal Memoir
Geoffrey Iley
A boy writes home during WWII, revealing his own fascinating
story, full of zest for life, information and humour.
Paperback: 978-1-78279-504-9 ebook: 978-1-78279-503-2

The Life & Times of the Real Robyn Hoode
Mark Olly
A journey of discovery. The chronicles of the genuine historical
character, Robyn Hoode, and how he became one of England's
greatest legends.
Paperback: 978-1-78535-059-7 ebook: 978-1-78535-060-3

Readers of ebooks can buy or view any of these bestsellers by clicking on the live link in the title. Most titles are published in paperback and as an ebook. Paperbacks are available in traditional bookshops. Both print and ebook formats are available online.

Find more titles and sign up to our readers' newsletter at
http://www.johnhuntpublishing.com/history-home

Follow us on Facebook at
https://www.facebook.com/ChronosBooks

and Twitter at https://twitter.com/ChronosBooks